Adventures in Modeling

Exploring Complex, Dynamic Systems with StarLogo

Vanessa Stevens Colella

Eric Klopfer

Mitchel Resnick

with illustrations by
Michelle Hlubinka

TEACHERS COLLEGE PRESS

Teachers College
Columbia University
New York and London

Published by Teachers College Press, 1234 Amsterdam Avenue, New York, NY 10027

Library of Congress Cataloging-in-Publication Data

Colella, Vanessa Stevens.
    Adventures in Modeling: Exploring Complex, Dynamic Systems with StarLogo /
      Vanessa Stevens Colella, Eric Klopfer, Mitchel Resnick.
        p. cm.
    Includes bibliographical references.
    ISBN 0-8077-4082-9 (pbk.)
      1. Computer simulation. 2. StarLogo (Computer program language) I. Klopfer, Eric.
II. Resnick, Mitchel.
QA76.9.C65 C63 2000
003'.35133—dc21

                    2001027324

ISBN 0-8077-4082-9

Contents

Acknowledgements

The ideas in this book emerged from our interactions with a vibrant community of educators and researchers. In particular, we would like to thank:

Molly Jones, for her unusual maturity, remarkable commitment, and keen insight.

Andrew Begel and Brian Silverman, for their technical wizardry, good cheer, and endless contributions.

The Santa Fe Institute, especially Ellen Goldberg, Ginger Richardson, and Andi Sutherland. The participants and leaders of the StarLogo Workshops in Santa Fe and Boston, especially James Taylor, Richard Noll, Larry Latour, Nigel Snoad, and Gil Munden. We would also like to thank Timothy Hely, Alfred Hubler, Melanie Mitchell, and Erik van Nimwegen.

The members and friends of the Lifelong Kindergarten group at the MIT Media Laboratory, especially, Rick Borovoy, Adam Eames, Sumita Kumar, Monica Linden, Fred Martin, Ankur Mehta, Bakhtiar Mikhak, Matt Notowidigdo, Randal Pinkett, Max Planck, David Williamson Shaffer, Carolyn Stoeber, Bill Thies, Diane Willow, Alice Yang, and Julie Yoo.

Bill Barowy, Linda Booth-Sweeney, Richard Elmore, Allan Feldman, Mark Guzdial, Janet Kolodner, Joe Krajcik, Frank Levy, Marcia Linn, Niall Palfreyman, Nancy Roberts, Bish Sanyal, Brian Smith, Elliot Soloway, John Sterman, Michael Tempel, and Sheldon White — for providing encouragement, advice, and assistance along the way.

British Telecommunications (especially Graham Cosier, Pat Hughes, and Steve Whitaker), the National Science Foundation, the LEGO Company, and the Media Laboratory research consortia for their intellectual interest and financial support. Nicholas Negroponte, the founder of the MIT Media Laboratory, for creating a research lab that inspires playful exploration and innovation.

On a personal note, we would also like to thank Giovanni Colella, Rachel Klopfer, John, Dale, and Grant Stevens, Fredda and Michael Klopfer, Simon and Carole Levin, and Shirley and Martin Resnick for their love and support.

About the Authors

Vanessa Stevens Colella worked on this book as a doctoral candidate in the Lifelong Kindergarten Group at the MIT Media Laboratory, where she investigated how innovative computational tools can transform the processes of teaching and learning. Vanessa was a charter corps member of Teach For America and taught junior high and high school science in East Los Angeles, Brooklyn, and Manhattan. She lives with her husband in San Francisco, California and will be joining McKinsey and Company in August 2001.

Eric Klopfer is the director of the Teacher Education Program and Assistant Professor of Science Education at MIT. Formerly a researcher in ecological complexity and technology coordinator for the Amherst, Massachusetts Public Schools, he now studies how people can learn about complex phenomena through simulations. He lives with his wife in North Andover, Massachusetts.

Mitchel Resnick is a professor (and playful inventor) at the MIT Media Laboratory, where he develops new technologies to help people (particularly children) learn new things in new ways. He developed the original version of StarLogo modeling software, and his research group developed ideas and technologies underlying the LEGO MindStorms robotics construction kit. He is co-founder of the Computer Clubhouse, a network of after-school learning centers for youth from underserved communities.

About the Designer

Michelle Hlubinka produces her colorful illustrations and layouts as a freelance graphic designer for various educational publishers and developers. She also creates imaginative calendars featuring her character, Binka, in farflung adventures, as well as small art books. She lives in Cambridge, Massachusetts.

Introduction

For thousands of years, people have been creating models to help them better understand the world around them. Leonardo DaVinci built models of flying machines that some claim were inspired by his desire to understand the flight of birds. Sir Isaac Newton described the behavior of physical systems with sets of equations. Jacques Vaucanson built a mechanical duck that actually ingested (and eliminated!) its food (Bedini, 1964). These models not only helped their creators better understand the phenomena that they were studying, but also helped them convey their new ideas to other people.

Throughout history, most people, like the pioneers mentioned above, have created models out of wood, paper, metal, and mathematical expressions. In more recent times, computers have provided a new medium for building, analyzing, and describing models. Using computers, economists build models of the stock market, biologists build models of cell division, and historians build models of ancient civilizations. Computers also make it easier for novices to build and explore their own models—and learn new scientific ideas in the process.

Research has shown that the process of creating models (as opposed to simply using models built by someone else) not only fosters model-building skills but also helps develop a greater understanding of the concepts embedded in the models (Confrey & Doerr, 1994; diSessa, 1986; Talsma, 2000). When you build your own models, you can decide what topic you want to study and how you want to study it. As your investigation proceeds, you can determine which aspects of the system you want to focus on, and refine your model as your understanding of the system grows. Perhaps most important, building your own models helps you develop a sound understanding of both how a system works and why it works that way.

The StarLogo language was designed to enable people to build their own models of complex, dynamic systems. Unlike many other modeling tools, StarLogo supports a tangible process of building, analyzing, and describing models that does not require advanced mathematical or programming skills. Using StarLogo, you can build and explore models—and in the process you can develop a deeper understanding of patterns and processes in the world around you.

New technologies, like StarLogo, can shape both what and how people learn. But, too often, people mistakenly believe that the mere presence of a new technology will be sufficient to cause change. The ability to learn new ideas through computer simulations, for example, is greatly influenced not only by the technologies used but also by the ways in which the simulations are presented. Creating an environment that supports learners' intellectual curiosity is just as important as providing the tools for building and exploring new phenomena. The open-ended Challenges and Activities in this book help you create such an environment by providing a means for understanding complex systems through the design and creation of your own dynamic models.

CREATING MODELS

During the past 10 years, simulation modeling, especially as it helps people to understand complex systems, has become a mainstream use of computational technology. The widespread popularity of "edutainment" software like SimCity and Civilization gives a clear indication of the extent to which simulation games have permeated popular culture. While it can be useful to experiment with prebuilt models like SimCity, a deeper understanding comes through building and manipulating models whose underlying structure is accessible (Feurzeig & Roberts, 1999; Resnick, Bruckman, & Martin, 1996). Just as a young child learns more by building a bridge out of blocks instead of merely playing with a prefabricated bridge, designing and creating your own models provide richer learning experiences than simply playing with prebuilt models. This learning process is critically important in domains that require an understanding of complex systems, from economics and mathematics to physics and biology. In addition, this learning process fosters the kinds of higher-order thinking and problem-solving skills that are called for in science, mathematics, and technology standards. This book focuses on learning about complex systems and developing the ability to create your own models in StarLogo, from the conceptualization of an idea through the final implementation, analysis, and presentation of a model.

Several common modeling programs, including Model-It, Stella, and MatLab, enable the design and creation of your own models. To model a system in one of these environments, you need to describe how the entire system changes. StarLogo approaches model building from a different perspective. In StarLogo, you write simple rules for individual behaviors. For instance, you might create rules for a bird that describe how fast it should fly and when it should fly towards another bird. When you watch many birds simultaneously following those rules, you can observe how patterns in the system, like flocking, arise out of the individual behaviors. Building up models from the individual, or "bird," level enables you to develop a better understanding of the system, or "flock," level behaviors.

While building your own models can be a great learning experience, it raises many questions about what to include in your model. We have found that people new to model building often believe that a model is only "good" or "useful" when it incorporates every possible aspect of a system. It is important to keep in mind that, even in the scope of "scientific modeling," people build a wide variety of models that encompass varying levels of detail and utilize a variety of methods. Depending on the goals you have, some approaches to model building will be more suitable than others. Choosing the one that best suits your personal goals and ideas can be a tricky process. Chapter 2 provides a framework for thinking about which approach is most appropriate for a particular set of goals.

INTERDISCIPLINARY NATURE

In recent years, there has been a surge of interest in the study of complex systems—that is, systems in which complex patterns and behaviors arise from simple rules and interactions. Researchers who study complex systems model economics as well as ecology, chemistry as well as population dynamics. Similarly, this book is not directed toward any single discipline. In StarLogo, you can model the dynamics of predator-prey relationships or experiment with the formation of traffic jams; you can investigate the demographics of neighboring countries or explore the collective behavior of groups of ants. Employing the principles covered in this book, you can design and create dynamic, complex models of systems from a variety of disciplines.

The conceptual organization of this book encourages you to draw on many perspectives as you create and analyze models. Consider a model of a rain forest. A biologist might study the model with an eye towards the interactions among the individuals, while an environmental chemist might focus on the accumulation of pollutants in different groups of creatures, and a mathematician might investigate the patterns of population growth and decline. Integrating these perspectives in both the creation and investigation phases of model building can enrich your models and help illuminate the underlying connections between seemingly disparate fields.

STRUCTURED EXPLORATION

One of our primary motivations when we wrote this book was to achieve a balance between structure and exploration. We designed the materials in this book to foster an exploratory, creative spirit while at the same time providing adequate structure for learning how to build models. In our experience, novices find this structured exploration to be engaging and more tractable than either didactic or completely open-ended learning environments.

The core of this book is a series of Activities and Challenges. Each Challenge is a problem statement intended to get your creative juices flowing. The Challenges encourage you to explore model design and construction while learning about the principles of complex systems. At the same time, they build familiarity with the StarLogo environment. The Challenges provide specific programming information when it is needed, thus minimizing the need for direct instruction or a lengthy manual. By structuring each Challenge to focus on key concepts, like how to move creatures or use variables, this book enables everyone to cultivate model-building skills in StarLogo.

Though "on-screen" computer modeling is one focus of this book, "off-screen" Activities provide another way to connect abstract notions of dynamic processes and complexity to personal experience. Participation in life-sized simulations helps learners develop deeper understandings of dynamic systems (Colella, 2000). The group Activities in the book allow participants to think about concepts like exponential growth, local versus global information, and group decision making from a personal perspective. Integrating the group Activities with the Challenges is an excellent way to learn about building models and exploring their content.

AUDIENCE

We designed this book primarily for educators. We use the term "educator" in its broadest sense. Whether you are teaching yourself, students, teachers, or your own child, you can use this book as an introduction to model building. This text can also provide an opportunity to learn about and implement new ways of teaching and learning. This book emphasizes the design and creation of modeling projects in an environment that promotes the exploration and explanation of new ideas. In addition, this book provides an innovative structure for teaching concepts from specific subject areas. By incorporating modeling into your classes, you and your students can gain new perspectives on important ideas and build deeper understandings of domain-specific content.

This book can be used in a variety of settings. For example, a ninth-grade social studies teacher can use it to enhance a unit on demographics. A professor can use it as a main or supplemental text in a course at a graduate school of education. Parents can use it to explore innovative uses of computers with their children. A boys and girls club mentor can use it to teach kids about scientific investigation through model construction and analysis. Workshop leaders can use it in a professional development seminar to draw connections between using technology and addressing the new science standards. As these examples illustrate, this book can be used in a wide variety of settings, not just to teach StarLogo, but also to incorporate facets of modeling into more traditional subjects or to provide the foundation for interdisciplinary explorations. In other words, this book is a flexible resource that can be applied in many environments.

ORGANIZATION

This book consists of three main sections. The first six chapters explain the philosophy behind StarLogo, introduce modeling concepts, describe the book structure, propose several different ways to use this book, and give a quick tour of the StarLogo world. The Activities and Challenges in the second section form the core of the Adventures curriculum. The Activities are group exercises that help participants gain a first-person perspective on complex, dynamic models. The Challenges are sequential lessons that help people develop both model-building skills and a better understanding of complex systems. Just after the Activities and Challenges, you will find Student Handouts for each Challenge. Finally, the appendices in the last section of the book contain notes about MacStarLogo, collected hints from the Challenges, and an explanation of common StarLogo error messages.

Travels with StarLogo

There is an old saying that goes something like this: "Give a person a hammer, and the whole world looks like a nail." Indeed, the ways we see the world are deeply influenced by the tools that we use.

For centuries, educators have used many different tools to help their students learn. When developing his concept of kindergarten in the early 1800s, Friedrich Froebel gave children a set of objects, which he called "gifts," to stimulate certain kinds of exploration (Brosterman, 1997). For example, colored balls and blocks encouraged children to explore shape and color. Montessori extended many of Froebel's ideas, creating materials that are still found in many elementary classrooms today.

Just as different Froebel gifts help children explore different concepts, different computer programs support different types of explorations and learning. The use of StarLogo in this book influences the types of projects that you work on. Even more important, it influences the type of thinking you do as you work on those projects.

StarLogo is designed especially for helping people create models of *decentralized systems*—that is, systems in which patterns arise from interactions among lots of individual objects. For example, StarLogo is well designed for exploring how bird flocks arise from interactions among individual birds, or how traffic jams arise from interactions among individual cars.

Decentralized systems are very common in the world. But it turns out that most people have great difficulty understanding the workings of such systems. That's why we see StarLogo as such a powerful tool. With StarLogo, you can create models of many phenomena that are familiar and important but traditionally difficult to understand.

In this chapter, we will give a brief introduction to the StarLogo approach to modeling—and the new ways of thinking that are nurtured by this type of modeling.

THE CENTRALIZED MINDSET

A flock of birds sweeps across the sky. How do birds keep their movements so orderly, so synchronized? Most people assume that birds play a game of Follow the Leader: The bird at the front of the flock leads, and the others follow. But that's not so. Most bird flocks don't have leaders at all. Rather, each bird follows a set of simple rules, reacting to the movements of the nearby birds. Orderly flocking patterns arise from these simple, local interactions. The bird in front is not a "leader" in any meaningful sense—it just happens to end up there. The flock is organized without an organizer, coordinated without a coordinator.

So why do most people assume that bird flocks have leaders? The problem extends beyond bird flocks. When people see patterns in the world, they tend to assume that someone or something is in charge of creating the pattern. When people see traffic jams, for example, they tend to assume an overturned truck or a broken bridge must be at fault; in fact, many traffic jams are caused by simple interactions among neighboring cars.

This tendency to assume centralized control, which we call the *centralized mindset*, makes it difficult for people to understand the workings of many phenomena in the world. The recurrent questioning of evolutionary theories is another example: When people see complex living systems in the world, they assume that someone or something must have explicitly designed them; instead, these livings systems are the products of millions of incremental changes over time. Both experts and novices fall into the centralized mindset. Until recently, even scientists assumed that bird flocks must have leaders. A similar bias toward centralized theories can be seen throughout the history of science.

One of the goals of StarLogo is to help people move beyond the centralized mindset, helping them learn how patterns can arise from lots of simple interactions among simple objects, without any object in charge. With StarLogo, you can model (and gain insights into) many real-life phenomena, such as bird flocks, traffic jams, ant colonies, and market economies. By writing simple rules for individual creatures, you are able to investigate the collective behavior of systems consisting of thousands of creatures. StarLogo models often exhibit behaviors at the system level that are not evident in the rules you write for individual behavior. These system-level behaviors are referred to as *emergent* because they arise out of the interactions among individuals. For instance, an ant colony can exhibit coordinated behavior as it forages for food, even though the rules describe only individual behavior, not colony-level behavior.

TOOLS FOR DECENTRALIZED THINKING

People already have lots of experience with decentralized systems; they observe decentralized systems all the time. But observation does not necessarily lead to deep understanding: People observed bird flocks for thousands of years before anyone suggested that flocks are leaderless. To develop a deeper understanding, people need opportunities not just to observe decentralized systems but to design their own models of decentralized systems.

Scientists have developed a variety of computational tools for this type of decentralized modeling. But most of these tools are designed for people with advanced mathematical or programming experience. StarLogo is an exception: It is designed explicitly for nonexperts.

StarLogo is an extension of Logo, a programming language that is generally used in elementary and secondary schools (Papert, 1980). In traditional versions of Logo, children create geometric patterns and animations by giving commands to a graphical *turtle* on the computer screen. The Logo turtle can be used to represent any type of object in the world: An ant, a car, a molecule. But traditional versions of Logo typically have only a few turtles. To support decentralized modeling, StarLogo has thousands of turtles, and all of the turtles can perform their actions at the same time, in parallel. Moreover, StarLogo turtles have better "senses" so that they can detect things (such as other turtles) in their local environment. Finally, the turtles' world is divided into small square sections called *patches*. For example, each patch can grow "food," which the turtles can search for and eat.

Unlike many other modeling programs, StarLogo allows you to directly observe both individual actions and the group patterns that emerge from those actions. The spatial nature of the program and its visual representation enable you to look at things (like creatures and their environment) instead of just looking at abstractions of things (like equations or graphs). This presentation of a model makes it easier to interpret what is happening. StarLogo makes it possible for everyone—even people without an extensive background in mathematics or programming—to design and build their own models.

AN EXAMPLE: TURTLE ECOLOGY

The legendary baseball manager Casey Stengel once said, "If you don't know where you're going, you might end up somewhere else." Our experiences with computer-based modeling activities have taught us a corollary: "Even if you think you know where you're going, you'll probably end up somewhere else."

That's what happened to Benjamin, a high school student, when he set out to create a StarLogo program that would simulate evolution by natural selection. At the core of Benjamin's simulation were turtles and food. His basic idea was simple: Turtles who eat a lot of food reproduce, and turtles who don't eat enough food die. Eventually, he planned to add "genes" to his turtles. Different genes could provide turtles with different levels of "fitness" (perhaps different capabilities for finding food). But, as often happens in the course of building models, Benjamin became fascinated by the fundamental behaviors that his model generated. On the road to evolution, Benjamin embarked on an interesting exploration of ecological systems (in particular, predator-prey systems).

Benjamin began by making food grow randomly throughout the StarLogo world. Then he created some turtles. The turtles had very meager sensory capabilities. They could not "see" or "smell" food at a distance. They could sense food only when they bumped directly into it. So the turtles followed a very simple strategy: Wander around randomly, eating whatever food you bump into.

Benjamin gave each turtle an energy level. Every time a turtle ate some food, its energy increased. Every time it took a step, its energy decreased a bit—and if its energy dipped to zero, it died. As he ran his model, Benjamin observed that sometimes all of the turtles died. After some experimenting, Benjamin added reproduction to his model: Whenever a turtle's energy increased above a certain threshold, the turtle "cloned" itself and split its energy with its new twin.

Benjamin assumed that his new rule for cloning would somehow balance the rule for dying, leading to some sort of equilibrium and preventing the extinction of his turtles. Benjamin started the model running again. But the rules didn't balance out as Benjamin had predicted—the turtle population repeatedly grew and declined. Meanwhile, the amount of available food also fluctuated, but out of phase with the turtles.

On each cycle, the turtles overgrazed the food supply, leading to a scarcity of food, and many of the turtles died. But then, with fewer turtles left to eat the food, the food became more abundant. The few surviving turtles thus found a plentiful food supply, and each of them rapidly increased its energy. When a turtle's energy surpassed a certain threshold, it cloned, increasing the turtle population. But as the population grew too high, food again became scarce, and the cycle started again. Visually, the oscillations were striking (see plot below). Turtles and food were always present, but the density of each continually changed.

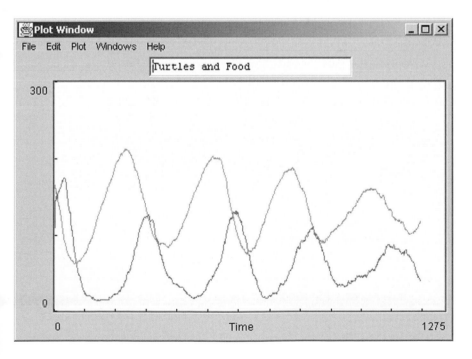

A Plot Window showing the changing densities of turtles and food.

The oscillating behavior in Benjamin's project is characteristic of ecological systems with predators (in this case, turtles) and prey (in this case, food). Traditionally, scientific (and educational) explorations of predator-prey systems are based on sets of differential equations, known as the Lotka-Volterra equations (see box at left). It is a straightforward matter to write a computer program based on those equations that computes how the population densities of the predators and prey vary with time.

This approach is typical of the way that scientists have traditionally modeled and studied the behaviors of all types of systems (physical, biological, and social). Scientists write down sets of equations and then attempt to solve them either analytically or numerically. Approaches like this one require advanced mathematical training—training that is usually available only at the university level.

The StarLogo approach to modeling systems (exemplified by Benjamin's predator-prey project) is sharply different. StarLogo makes systems-related ideas much more accessible to students by providing them with a stronger personal connection to the underlying models. Traditional differential-equation approaches are "impersonal" in two ways. The first is obvious: They rely on abstract symbol manipulation (accessible only to people with advanced mathematical training). The second is more subtle: Differential equations deal in aggregate quantities. In the Lotka-Volterra system, for example, the differential equations describe how the overall populations (not the individual creatures) change over time. There are now some very good computer modeling tools—such as Stella and Model-It—that are based on differential equations. These tools eliminate the need to manipulate symbols, focusing on more qualitative and graphical descriptions. But they still rely on aggregate quantities.

In StarLogo, by contrast, students think about the actions and interactions of individual objects or creatures. StarLogo projects describe how individual creatures (not overall populations) behave. Thinking in terms of individual creatures seems far more intuitive and is accessible to students of all levels. Students can imagine themselves as individual creatures and think about what they might do in a certain situation. By describing and observing the dynamics at the level of the individual creatures, rather than at the aggregate level of population densities, students can more easily think about and understand the patterns that arise. Just as Benjamin charted a new path to understanding, this book will enable you to explore new territory and, perhaps, view the world a little differently.

CHAPTER 2

Models in Science and Education

Creating your own models can be a powerful learning experience. But where do you start? Perhaps the most important question to consider when building any kind of model is, "What purpose will my model serve?" Is it intended to help you explore a new topic or gain a better understanding of a phenomenon that you have observed? Do you want to show someone an instantiation of an idea that you have been thinking about or display the data that you have collected in a particular investigation? All of these (and many others) are valid reasons to build models. Thinking through your goals at the outset helps you structure the process of creating your model.

Once you have thought about why you want to build a model, you will need to determine what kind of model to build. Different kinds of models serve different purposes. Before looking specifically at creating models in StarLogo, this chapter describes a few different types of scientific models. This discussion provides some background for building your own scientific models.

TYPES OF MODELS

What is a scientific model? Most people have experience with models that illustrate scientific phenomena. Like the dioramas of elementary school days, these *illustrative* models are meant to provide some kind of visualization of a scientific process or system. Models of this type include models of the solar system that show the planetary orbits, paper models of DNA chains that can be manipulated to show DNA replication or transcription, and transparent human bodies that show all of the internal organs. All of these examples are models because they capture an aspect of a scientific system or process—and help you understand it in new ways.

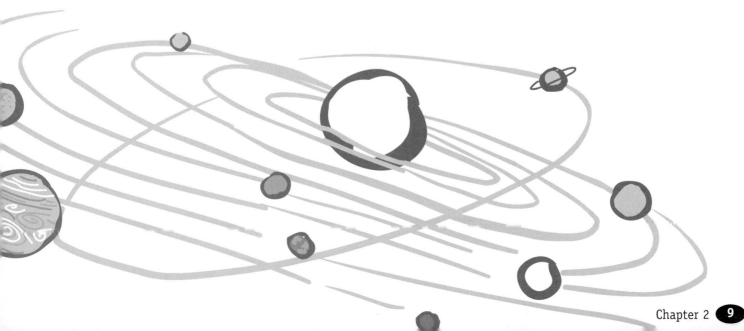

But a physics student would probably think very differently about the question, "What is a scientific model?" She might explain that $x = \frac{1}{2}at^2$ is a model of how position depends on acceleration and time. An economics professor might discuss a model of supply and demand that is described by equations. These kinds of models, which are based on mathematical equations and enable exploration of a variety of scenarios, comprise a second category of scientific models—*analytical* models. Analytical models generate solutions that predict behaviors of systems based on a given set of conditions. For instance, using the equation $x = \frac{1}{2}at^2$ you can determine position (x) for any values of acceleration (a) and time (t). While fewer people have experience with analytical models, they are critical in many types of activities such as forecasting economic cycles and predicting demographic trends.

In the past two decades, the growing presence of computers has ushered in a new approach to modeling. Many illustrative and analytical models can be constructed on computers, enabling people to study more complex problems than they could without the aid of computers. But computers also opened the door for another category of models, called *simulation* models, that would be difficult if not impossible to create without computers. In a simulation model, rather than solving equations, you describe the underlying mechanisms and let them *run* over time to see what happens. With simulation models, it is easier to incorporate random and probabilistic events, reflecting important aspects of the world around us. These properties of simulation models enable some explorations that are difficult to accomplish with analytical models (and impossible to show in illustrative models). Moreover, the flexible, intuitive nature of simulation models makes building them accessible to students of all levels. There are many kinds of simulation models, ranging from models that help people forecast weather to those that help people understand large-scale ecosystem effects.

Many phenomena can be represented by all three types of models. For example, if you wanted to build an illustrative model of the probability of getting all heads when flipping four coins, you could draw pictures of all of the possible outcomes of heads and tails with four coins. If you were building an analytical model of the same game, you could use equations to calculate the probability of getting heads four times in a row. In a simulation model, you could run a "four-coin" simulation and observe how often you got all heads. (And, in a simulation model, your results are not likely to be exactly the same every single time you run it.)

DEFINING YOUR SIMULATION MODEL

StarLogo is one platform for building simulation models. In StarLogo you build up complex behaviors from simple rules. The dynamic nature of StarLogo simulations allows for a kind of iterative exploration that you are unlikely to replicate in a classic illustrative model. And StarLogo enables you to define relationships among individuals in the system without using complex mathematical equations like those typically employed in analytical models.

There are many challenges in constructing your own simulation models. The open-ended nature of the StarLogo program gives you extensive flexibility but provides little direction as to the kinds of things that should be included in various models. As you work on a project, you may be uncertain about what to add to your model or unsure about how to pare down an overly complex model.

There is another way to distinguish models that can be useful as you plan and construct your own models. This classification scheme, proposed by Roughgarden, differentiates models according to their purpose and the amount of real-world complexity that they incorporate (Roughgarden, Bergman, Shafir, & Taylor, 1996). Roughgarden defines three such categories of models—"minimal models for an idea," "minimal models for systems," and "systems models." Just as deciding whether you want to build an illustrative, analytical, or simulation model can help you take the first step in defining your project, making choices about your model based on Roughgarden's taxonomy can help you define the scope of your project.

The first type of model, *minimal models for an idea* or *idea models*, seeks to capture only the most fundamental parts of the system, without incorporating a high level of detail. Often, idea models are used to illustrate a general principle. The most useful idea models are those that strip away as much extraneous information as possible and boil things down to the most relevant parts. For example, you can create idea models of predator-prey relationships, supply and demand, and molecular motion.

The second type of model, *minimal models for a system*, attempts to incorporate some aspects of an actual system without incorporating a fine level of detail about the system. A minimal model includes enough specificity to narrow the applicability of the model without including so much detail that it only applies to one particular case. These models represent generalized systems, like herbivores grazing on a grassy landscape or storeowners pricing baked goods.

The third type of model, *systems models*, simulates an actual system with as much detail as possible. These models are usually built as a collaborative effort among many researchers, each gathering different details about a system and together synthesizing their findings into a huge model. Systems models require extensive data collection and intensive effort. A model of the growth, movement, and interactions of all of the plants and animals in Yellowstone National Park is a systems model. Models like this one often take years to build, even with the participation of many experts.

To clarify the differences among these model types, consider a model of population growth and how it might be modified to fit into each of the three classes. A model of population growth that could apply to any kind of living creature would be an idea model. If you added enough detail so that the model only applied to carnivorous animals, it would be a minimal model for a system. Finally, if you collected and incorporated data on a single pack of wolves in Alaska, along with specific information about the prey that they hunt, the environment in which they live, and their relationships with one another, it would be a systems model.

BUILDING YOUR MODEL IN STARLOGO

StarLogo is designed primarily to facilitate the construction of simulation models, rather than illustrative or analytical models. And StarLogo is best suited for the construction of idea models. It is certainly possible to build a minimal systems model in StarLogo, but it is almost always preferable to begin by constructing an idea model and later expand upon that model if you feel it is useful. It is important to recognize that more detail does not result in a better model, it simply results in a different kind of model. Think about the aspects of the model that you are really interested in and remember that the complexity of a model grows exponentially as you add more variables. Your challenge in defining your project is not to make it as complex and realistic as possible but to incorporate only those concepts that help you develop a clear understanding of the system. Models that focus on a core set of ideas are often better learning tools, both for the builder and the user.

With StarLogo, you can build your own models, not just explore other people's models. There are many benefits to building your own models: You can decide what topic you want to investigate; you can control the underlying rules that govern your model; you can alter the behavior that your model generates; and you can make connections between your model's behavior and the underlying mechanisms. In short, you can develop a deep understanding of the phenomenon you have chosen to explore.

CHAPTER 3
Planning Your Adventure

Like a trek through the Australian outback or a journey to the islands of the Galapagos, your Adventures with StarLogo will enable you to see the world in new ways. But like any adventure, you will probably want to do some planning before you embark on your journey. This chapter gives an overview of what lies ahead and suggests a number of possible itineraries for your StarLogo Adventure. We will provide some information for the Adventurer: You will discover when you need to "pack" your computer and when you can leave home without it. You will also become acquainted with the feature attractions of your Adventure—Challenges and Activities. You will learn about the Challenge structure and how you can use the projects to explore both modeling concepts and more traditional subject matter. You will also learn about the Activities and how they can be combined with the Challenges to create a powerful learning experience. Finally, you will become acquainted with a set of tools and techniques for leading a successful Adventure.

CHALLENGES

The Challenges are the pillars of this book. They help learners become familiar with the StarLogo environment and introduce them to the principles of modeling complex, dynamic systems. Each Challenge poses an open-ended problem and gives you the tools to design and create a solution in StarLogo. We structured the Challenges to embrace a wide variety of solutions and enable you to build coherent and interesting models, even before your developing knowledge of the StarLogo language is complete. The Challenges contain programming hints and pointers for sample projects, which illustrate implementations of the key concepts in the Challenge. This format minimizes the need for direct instruction. Exploring the Challenges helps learners build a repertoire of modeling skills and a command of the StarLogo language.

To get the most out of the Challenges, explore them in StarLogo rather than just reading through them. We strongly suggest that if you are teaching with this book, you complete the Challenges yourself, preferably before you present them to your students. Every Challenge comes with associated StarLogo projects (in the Adventures Projects folder installed with StarLogo). Though these projects are also described in the text, you will learn more by exploring them in StarLogo. It might be helpful to skim the Challenge ahead of time (especially the Challenge statement, the Challenge Philosophy, and the Tips for Teachers), but we suggest that you pursue the Challenges while you are at a computer and are able to experiment directly with the Challenge concepts.

Each Challenge is divided up into the following sections:	
Challenge	Gives a brief statement of the modeling problem or design goal of the Challenge.
Possible Explorations	Provides a range of extended activities to pursue, each of which relates to the Challenge.
Modeling Concepts	Describes the modeling principles that are addressed in the Challenge.
StarLogo Concepts	Describes the key StarLogo ideas that are introduced in the Challenge.
Challenge Philosophy	Situates the Challenge within a broader modeling context.
Challenge Description	Provides further details about the goal of the Challenge.
Challenge Guidelines	Supplies specific StarLogo programming information and illustrates possible Challenge solutions or related ideas with sample projects.
Tips for Teachers	Concludes the Challenge with a recap of major concepts covered and evaluation tips for teachers.

Each Challenge contains a lot of information. We do not suggest that you hand out the entire chapter to your students, unless your students are going to be teaching with this book at a later date, in which case they should have their own copy of the text. For other students, we have included Student Handouts for each Challenge, which contain the Challenge statement, the Possible Explorations, and some hints from the Challenge Guidelines. The Student Handouts also contain short descriptions of the sample Adventures Projects. You can integrate the other information from the Challenges, including the philosophy behind the Challenge, analogies to real systems, and evaluation criteria, into discussions with your students.

Before handing out the student materials, it is often useful to introduce the main modeling and StarLogo concepts. Because the relevant programming information is contained in the Challenges, it is not necessary, and can be counterproductive, to deliver a lengthy introduction. We have found that demonstrating some of the features of a single sample project can be an effective introductory technique. In some of the later Challenges, you can begin with an exploration of real-world systems that exhibit some of the interactions you are modeling.

When you present students with the Challenge, you will find that their learning styles vary—some like to jump right into the Challenge by starting their own project from scratch, while others prefer to explore and modify the sample projects. Both approaches work well. Challenges that require the use of particular sample projects indicate that requirement in the Challenge statement.

ACTIVITIES

The Activities provide an alternate perspective on many of the modeling principles that are covered in this book. The Activities engage groups of people in life-sized simulations, enabling you and your students to participate in and "see inside of" a dynamic system (Booth Sweeney & Meadows, forthcoming 2001). These group exercises help participants draw connections between computer models of complex systems and their own real-life experiences with similar systems. When interwoven with the Challenges, they provide an opportunity to explore modeling from different perspectives, appealing to different learning styles.

Each Activity is divided up into the following sections:	
Modeling Concepts	Describes the modeling ideas that are illustrated through the Activity.
Materials	Lists the items required to run the Activity.
Running the Activity	Designed for the instructor, explains how to conduct the Activity.
Facts for Facilitators	Provides additional tips for facilitating the Activity.

Unlike the Challenges, no part of the Activity write-ups should be handed out to students. Many of the Activities depend on inventing and adopting strategies during the Activity. The Activity write-ups often include information for the facilitator about optimal strategies for individuals, the underlying rules of the model, or the theoretical basis for the Activity. We find that the Activities are far more effective learning tools if the students are able to discover these principles through their experience during the Activity and subsequent discussion, rather than by reading about them ahead of time. If your students are pre-service or in-service teachers, ask them not to read the Activity until after you have conducted it. As a facilitator, it is best if you read the whole Activity ahead of time, and you might even try running it with a pilot group. None of the Activities requires the use of a computer.

The Activities and Challenges are interwoven in this book because they are complementary classroom exercises. The Activities use diverse materials to facilitate the exploration of agent-based modeling concepts from different perspectives and to foster a deeper understanding of individual and systemic behaviors. In most cases, the Activities and the Challenges are not explicitly linked to one another. In fact, unlike the Challenges, the Activities need not be conducted in any particular order. We do strongly suggest that you alternate between Activities and Challenges. This organization not only gives students an opportunity to reflect on what they are learning and to discuss the nature of dynamic systems, but also engages students with different learning styles. While the book presents the Activities in a particular order, it is fine to modify that order to accommodate your goals and constraints. (Note: The only exception is that Activity 3 should immediately precede Challenge 3.)

EMBARKING ON YOUR ADVENTURE

This book can be adapted for use in a variety of settings. We have already used the Challenges and Activities in graduate schools of education, high school and middle school classrooms, professional training programs, in-service professional development workshops, and after-school programs. We developed a set of pedagogical structures that enables you to use the Challenges and Activities in each of these environments. These structures include successive presentation of the Activities and Challenges, reflective discussion after the Activities, and informal discussions and group presentations during the Challenges.

The following section describes our own approach to conducting the Challenges and Activities within the framework created by this book. Throughout this section, we use the term "students" broadly, to include all participants from in-service teachers to middle school students but not the facilitator.

Conducting Activities and Challenges

Typically, we begin with an Activity. Before commencing the Activity, we give students instructions about the mechanics of the Activity, and we highlight particular behaviors, strategies, and dynamics, which they might want to watch for. The Activities themselves take between 10 and 30 minutes to conduct. First, we allow students to try the Activity once and then lead them in a discussion of their observations and initial ideas about the Activity. Following that discussion, we introduce an intervention (often students suggest valuable interventions) and allow them to rerun the Activity and observe the new dynamics. The post-activity discussions can be quite lengthy, so we try to gently direct the students towards the central concepts of the Activity. Often, the facilitator must decide when to wrap up these conversations. We typically close the Activity when we feel that all of the participants have explored the central concepts, though the goals and constraints of the setting influence the timing of that decision.

After the Activity, we introduce a Challenge. As discussed earlier, we find that a short description of the Challenge is often sufficient to get students started. We strongly recommend that students work on the Challenges in small groups. We allow students from one to two hours to complete a Challenge (the earlier Challenges often take less time). We often stretch a single Challenge over multiple days and engage students in Activities or other classroom exercises in between work on the Challenge. If students want to pursue a Challenge for more time, additional computer access outside of class is helpful. As students are working on the Challenges, we circulate around the room and check on the progress of each group. During these conversations, we ask students to describe what they want their models to show, reflect on how well their models achieve this goal, and think about the next steps that they want to take. We also assist students with technical or conceptual difficulties that they have encountered; however, we encourage them to seek help first from other groups.

About two-thirds of the way through each Challenge (though this can be done at the end of the Challenge, if necessary), we gather all of the students together and ask each group to make a brief presentation about an interesting facet of their model. These progress reports allow students to show their work without the pressure of presenting a final project. We pay special attention to how well their models communicate ideas to other people. After each group's presentation, the facilitators, guests, and other students all give feedback to the model builders, enabling them to revise and improve their models in the remaining class time.

Creating a Learning Environment

A key element to the success of exploring the Challenges and Activities in this book is creating the appropriate learning environment. Ideally, the environment should provide adequate freedom balanced with appropriate feedback. Adequate freedom can mean:

- Having enough time to fully explore the Challenges.

- Being able to pursue a variety of solutions to a single problem.

- Having ample physical space to diagram ideas.

- Enjoying opportunities to explore ideas through non-traditional learning activities.

- Being free to consult with peers and work in teams in a relaxed social environment.

Appropriate feedback can entail:

- Instituting mechanisms to provide constructive, generative suggestions.

- Facilitating peer-to-peer conversations about projects.

- Helping students make connections to underlying modeling and programming concepts.

- Discussing the goals of a project.

- Presenting projects to larger communities for external review.

There are many ways to engender this kind of environment, and, depending on your setting, it will undoubtedly be preferable to emphasize some aspects more than others.

Adapting the Architecture Design Studio

Architecture schools have a long history of structuring learning environments by using design challenges that are solved with input from classmates and teachers. We structure students' work on the Challenges similarly, by adapting two key components of the architecture design studio: A format for informal student-teacher interactions and the public presentation of work-in-progress (Colella, Klopfer, & Resnick, 1999). Incorporating these ideas can foster creative thinking and cognitive mastery, while at the same time providing a time-tested structure to support community-based learning through design tasks. We find that using informal student-teacher interactions and public presentations to organize the Challenges enable students to develop both the abilities to design, implement, and explore simulations and the facilities to describe, analyze, and critique simulations (Kafai & Ching, 1998; Kolodner, Crismond, Gray, Holbrook, & Puntambekar, 1998; Shaffer, 1998).

Though the Challenge structure outlined above has been very useful, we have found that the work-in-progress presentations can run too long (we try to keep the presentations to fewer than three minutes each, except for the final presentation of the semester or workshop). All types of "students," from younger children to experienced teachers, occasionally try to describe every aspect of their model instead of focusing on a specific idea or issue. To address this problem, we sometimes ask the groups to spend a few minutes presenting their work to another group instead of to the whole class. Alternatively, we ask students to write answers to a few focused questions before their presentations. The Tips for Teachers section of the Challenges can help you generate these questions.

Another way to prepare students for their presentations is to use the StarLogo Design Discussion Area (DDA), which is based on the work of Janet Kolodner and colleagues at Georgia Tech (Kolodner & Nagel, 1999; Puntambekar & Kolodner, 1998). This online resource provides a structure for people to record their ideas, share those ideas with others, and receive feedback on their original design efforts. The original DDA has been adapted for the StarLogo Adventures Challenges. You can use the DDA to facilitate discussions and presentations in your own class or to collaborate with StarLogo Adventurers in another class or in another country. It can also be used as a repository for student work and discussion. After reviewing this tool, you might choose to replace some of the classroom presentations with online summaries and student reviews. More information about this resource can be found online at http://education.mit.edu/starlogo/dda. You and your students can also use the starlogo-users@media.mit.edu mailing list to share your ideas and models. If you are willing to share your curriculum materials with others, then please contact us at starlogo-adventures@media.mit.edu so that we can arrange to put your work online.

Integrating Your Adventure

There is no need to make the Challenges and Activities the sole focus of a course. There are many ways in which these resources can be used in conjunction with other course materials. The Challenges and Activities might be packaged into a single unit during a course or interspersed throughout the semester (though, in our experience, doing the first few Challenges and Activities within a few weeks of each other accelerates students' learning). While the Challenges and Activities are fairly flexible, most learning environments have their own built-in constraints. In particular, integrating new materials into secondary school classes often requires additional planning. Chapter 5 presents a few ideas about integrating this book in a secondary school.

CHAPTER 4

Frequently Asked Questions

What kind of computer skills do I need?

While this book provides some instructions about basic computer operations, it does assume familiarity with a computer. If you are comfortable using a word processing program, creating images in a program like KidPix or Photoshop, or surfing the web on your computer, then your skills are adequate to begin your Adventure.

What kind of mathematical skills do I need?

While knowledge of complex mathematics is not required to build models in StarLogo, some mathematical and logical thinking skills are. StarLogo does require beginning knowledge of algebra and geometry to implement certain features in your models. We suggest that elementary-age children who are not yet familiar with these mathematical concepts start by exploring prebuilt StarLogo models (perhaps some that you create for them) or building their own models in another version of Logo, like MicroWorlds Logo (http://www.lcsi.ca).

What do I need to know about models or simulations?

This book is a great way to introduce yourself or your students to models and simulations. Our approach is not merely to present StarLogo mechanics, but to impart an understanding of the art and science of modeling. Of course, StarLogo is just one of many modeling environments. Previous experience with models or simulations can set your StarLogo exploration in a richer context, just as experience with StarLogo will enrich your understanding of the models that you encounter in the future.

Do I need to know how to program in StarLogo or another language?

No, this book begins with basic programming concepts, so you do not need previous programming experience.

Do I need one computer for each student?

No. We suggest that students work together on the Challenges. Groups of two or three students per computer are ideal. It is important that every student has time to play with StarLogo.

What kind of computer do I need?

There are both Java (cross-platform) and Macintosh-specific versions of StarLogo. This book was written for the Java version but can be used with MacStarLogo as well. If you are using a Mac, you can use either the Java version or MacStarLogo. We strongly recommend that you download the Java version if possible. If you are running StarLogo using Java on a PC, you need at least a Pentium 133. To run the Java version on a Mac, you need at least a G3 (all iMacs and iBooks have at least G3 processors). If you are running MacStarLogo you need a Quadra, Centris, or Performa 600 series or better. The 68K version needs 7 MB of free RAM and the PowerPC version needs 8.5 MB. Information specific to MacStarLogo can be found in Appendix A.

Can this book help my students and me meet the state and national curriculum standards?

While standards vary considerably from state to state, almost all of them call for encouraging students to engage in higher-order thinking and for integrating technology into mathematics and science courses (among others). Some states specifically call for the use of modeling and simulation in secondary classes. The Challenges and the Activities in this book can help you meet these standards. Though we cannot list all of the overlap between this book and the standards in your state, you can find some guidelines and examples in Chapter 5.

What size group of students can this book accommodate?

This book is best used in a course that allows for student-student interaction. It is not intended for use in a large, lecture-format class, unless smaller section meetings supplement the class. The Challenges work best in a class of fewer than 35 students. All of the Activities can accommodate at least 35 students and most work best with more than a dozen participants.

Can I use this book on my own or to teach an individual child?

While the Activities described in this book are intended for groups, the modeling Challenges can be explored on your own, with an individual child, or with a small group of students. If you or your students would like to interact with other StarLogo Adventurers, you can log onto the StarLogo Adventures website (http://www.media.mit.edu/starlogo/adventures) to share ideas, exchange questions, and post solutions. In addition, you can log onto the StarLogo Design Discussion Area (http://education.mit.edu/starlogo/dda), to receive feedback on your models and give others input on their work. If you are learning StarLogo by yourself, you might want to collaborate with other StarLogo users through the email list (starlogo-users@media.mit.edu). You may sign up for the mailing list by emailing starlogo-request@media.mit.edu or by visiting us online at http://www.media.mit.edu/starlogo/community/mailinglist.htm.

How do I get StarLogo?

StarLogo is on the CD that comes with this book and is also available for free on the web at http://www.media.mit.edu/starlogo. Click on download and choose whether you'd like the Java, PowerPC, or the 68K version. We strongly recommend that, if you can, you download the Java version. If you have an older version of StarLogo, please replace it with the latest version included on the CD or available online. When you download StarLogo, you will receive a folder of Sample Projects and a folder of Adventures Projects. In addition, all of the documentation for StarLogo is included in the download. We encourage you to sign up for the starlogo-users@media.mit.edu mailing list and share your experiences with other StarLogo users.

StarLogo Sites

http://www.media.mit.edu/starlogo/adventures	Adventures home page
http://www.media.mit.edu/starlogo	StarLogo home page
http://www.media.mit.edu/macstarlogo	MacStarLogo home page
http://education.mit.edu/starlogo/dda	Design Discussion Area for StarLogo
http://ccl.sesp.northwestern.edu/cm/starlogoT	StarLogoT page

State and National Standards

http://www.enc.org/professional/standards	Links to all national and state standards
http://putnamvalleyschools.org/Standards.html	Links to all state standards
http://www.achieve.org	Compare state standards by discipline
http://www.nctm.org/standards	NCTM mathematics standards
http://www.project2061.org	AAAS science standards
http://www.nap.edu/catalog/9596.html	NRC science standards

Related Activities

http://www.meas.ncsu.edu/outreach/fish_school.html	Schools are for Fish activities
http://www.red3d.com/cwr/boids	Boids home page by Craig Reynolds
http://www.taumoda.com/web/PD/setup.html	Evolution of Cooperation
http://el.www.media.mit.edu/groups/el/projects/emergence	Active essay on the Game of Life
http://www.media.mit.edu/~vanessa/part-sims	Information on Participatory Simulations

Other Modeling Environments

http://www.agentsheets.com	AgentSheets home page
http://www.lcsi.ca	Logo home page
http://hi-ce.eecs.umich.edu/sciencelaboratory	Model-It home page
http://www.hps-inc.com/stella/stella.htm	Stella home page
http://www.mathworks.com	MatLab home page

Institutions

http://www.media.mit.edu	MIT Media Laboratory
http://education.mit.edu	MIT Teacher Education Program
http://tc-press.tc.columbia.edu	Teachers College Press, Columbia University
http://www.santafe.edu	The Santa Fe Institute
http://www.bt.com	British Telecommunications, Inc.

Mailing Lists

starlogo-request@media.mit.edu	Help with StarLogo installation and errors
starlogo-users@media.mit.edu	Mailing list for all StarLogo users
starlogo-adventures@media.mit.edu	List for sharing curriculum and ideas

CHAPTER 5

Adventures in a Secondary School Environment

In this chapter, we outline several ways to integrate the material in this book into secondary school courses. First, we discuss tailoring the existing Challenges for a tighter fit with the content of a single course. Next, we discuss two modes of faculty collaboration. We describe a team approach in which a group of faculty members divides up the Challenges and coordinates their implementation, and we explore the value of simultaneously pursuing individual Challenges from different perspectives, enabling a multi-disciplinary approach to modeling. Finally, we present some examples describing how your Adventure can help you and your students meet state and national standards. There are countless ways to use this book, and we hope that these ideas spur you to think creatively about how you can use this material to introduce model design and creation to your students.

TAILORING YOUR ADVENTURE

You can modify Activities, Challenges, and sample projects to increase their applicability for particular courses or discipline-specific goals. Usually, this process involves adding constraints that encourage students to explore a particular set of interactions during the Activity or Challenge, or creating or modifying sample projects to give examples that are appropriate for a specific discipline. The following scenarios illustrate a range of adaptations to the Challenges.

Course: A.P. Physics

In Challenge 7, students learn more about turtle-turtle inter-actions. Students can use the "speed" variable and devise a way to investigate acceleration. Can they place other objects in the environment that affect the turtles' speed? What would happen to the turtles' speed if the students added gravity or friction to their StarLogo model? Modifying the sample project **Collisions** is a good way to explore some of these ideas.

Course: Introductory Biology

In Challenge 6, turtles begin to exchange information with one another. You can use this Challenge to enable students to explore the dynamics of disease transmission. The sample project *Epidemic* is an idea model of a contagious disease moving through a population. Can your students make modifications that incorporate other characteristics of disease transmission, like variable infectivity, environmental risks, mortality, "safe" zones, immunity, or vaccination? See http://www.media.mit.edu/starlogo/projects/diseases.html for some modifications of *Epidemic* that incorporate characteristics of specific diseases.

Course: Chemistry

Challenge 10 introduces special types or *breeds* of turtles. You can modify this Challenge to focus on different ways to catalyze chemical reactions. Students can create breeds of turtles that represent different molecules. The local presence of the "catalyst" turtles causes the reaction to proceed, as in the sample project *Enzyme*. Is there a threshold level of catalyst necessary to cause all of the turtles to react? Can the students model temperature and observe its effect on the reaction rate? Can they create a simulation of a catalyzed reversible reaction?

Course: Social Studies

Students explore graphing and data visualization in Challenge 8. Some of the later Challenges can easily be grouped together to enable a more in-depth exploration of a topic. You can ask students to build a model of population growth, create an "age" variable, and design rules for birth and death in their population. Then they can investigate the demographics of their population. How do the different population models in the class compare with one another? Ask students to investigate the effect of high levels of child mortality on their population. How do varying life spans affect their populations? During Challenge 8, can students build data visualizations to illustrate the patterns that they have identified in their population?

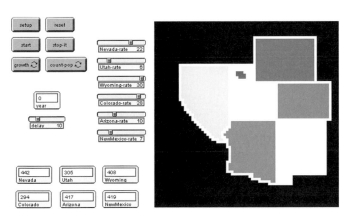

The Turtle Demographics project.

The Gaussian project.

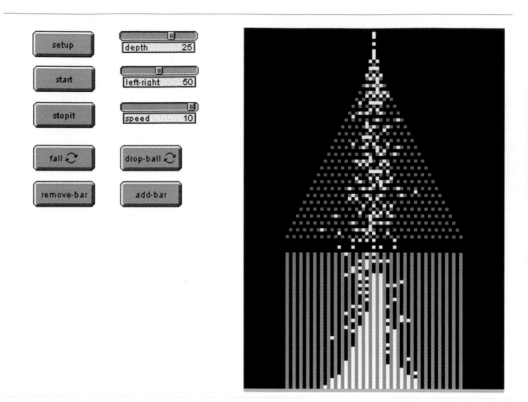

Course: Probability and Statistics

Challenge 4 asks students to construct a model in which turtles interact with the patches. This Challenge could be focused on creating patterns in the environment that cause the turtles to make choices based on probabilistic rules. The sample project **Gaussian** uses an environmental pattern and a simple probability-based decision rule to arrange the turtles in a normal distribution. Changing the probability alters the resulting distribution. Can your students create patterns that generate other distributions? Or devise another way to construct a normal distribution of turtles?

FACULTY COLLABORATION

Collaborations among faculty members are another way to maximize the benefit of this book for your students. These collaborations can take many forms. One strategy is to take a divide-and-conquer approach, distributing the Challenges and Activities among several teachers. This approach enables teachers to find the best fit between the Challenges and the content of each course. Not only does this arrangement reduce the amount of time spent learning StarLogo in each course, but it can also help the students build connections between their courses. Arrangements like this one can solidify working relationships among faculty members and support the development of cross-curricular projects.

An alternative to dividing the Challenges among the faculty is simultaneously pursuing a Challenge in several classes. Approaching a Challenge from multiple perspectives enables you to build explicit links between curricula and illustrates the connections between disciplines. For instance, a biology teacher, a mathematics teacher, and a social studies teacher can work together on a model of an ecosystem. Using the model, students can explore the relationships between different species in the ecosystem, observe the population trends generated by the ecosystem model and compare those trends to the curves generated by algebraic models, and analyze the economic, social, and biological implications of various land management and population control strategies. This method of interdisciplinary investigation can be a source of rich classroom discussion. Depending on the constraints of your institution, you might even find that building a unit around a single model, and exploring that model in a number of different classes, helps your students to build a deep understanding of important concepts. In our experience, even a short collaboration between teachers from different disciplines yields new understandings for all participants.

MEETING THE STANDARDS

As the move towards state and national standards grows, it is becoming increasingly important to tie classroom activities directly to the standards. While standards vary considerably from state to state, most call for engaging students in inquiry-based activities. In addition, many recommend integrating technology into the everyday explorations of all disciplines, and some stress the importance of incorporating modeling and simulation in secondary school courses. In particular, science, mathematics, and social studies standards explicitly address the need for student use and development of models. This book can help you address these general requirements. It can also help you meet other, more specific standards.

The growing length and number of standards make it impossible to provide a comprehensive treatment of all of the connections between the Adventures curriculum and all of the state and national standards. We strongly suggest that you look at **http://putnamvalleyschools.org/Standards.html** and **http://www.enc.org/professional/standard**. These websites provide links to all national and state standards. Also visit **http://www.achieve.org**, which allows you to search for standards specific to particular grade levels, subject areas, states, etc.

The following classroom examples illustrate some ways that this book helps address a wide range of learning goals. We encourage you to share other links between your Adventure and the standards that apply to your classes through the **starlogo-users@media.mit.edu** mailing list.

Educational experiences in grades 5–8 will assure that students...solve problems involving the concept of, calculation of, and relationships among length, perimeter, area, volume, angle measure, capacity, weight, mass, and temperature, and develop and use formulas and procedures for solving measurement problems.

Connecticut, Mathematics Content Standard 5,
5–8 Performance Standards

Students will use mathematical analysis, scientific inquiry, and engineering design, as appropriate, to pose questions, seek answers, and develop solutions...[They] will understand the relationships and common themes that connect mathematics, science, and technology and apply the themes to these and other areas of learning.

New York, Learning Standards for Mathematics, Science,
and Technology at Three Levels, Standards 1 and 6

[Students will] analyze factors that influence chemical and physical change; hypothesize the effect of variables on chemical reactions; experiment with variables affecting the relative rates of chemical and physical changes (e.g., temperature, stirring, crushing, concentration).

Utah, Science Secondary Core Curriculum Standards,
Eighth Grade Integrated Science,
Chemical Changes and Physical Change, Standard 3240–0102

All students will...relate various representations of concepts or procedures to one another... [and] apply mathematical thinking and modeling to solve problems that arise in other disciplines.

Massachusetts, Mathematics Content, Basic Education, Connections

Monica and Nigel's Melting Model

Monica and Nigel are middle school students. They are studying simple geometric shapes in math class and are starting to learn about the behavior of molecules in science. For science class, they built a StarLogo model to investigate whether or not the size of an ice cube influences the rate at which it melts. Building the first ice cube was easy—they drew one large ice cube in the middle of the screen. Then they created some turtles who wandered around randomly. Every time a turtle ran into an ice cube patch it "melted" a piece of the ice cube by turning the patch from blue to black. They used a stopwatch to determine how long it took the ice cube to melt completely.

Monica realized that they could simulate splitting the ice cube in half by drawing two smaller ice cube pieces, whose combined area was equal to that of the original ice cube. Once they created the right size ice cubes, they repeated their experiment and recorded the melting time. Now that they had a method for splitting the ice cube into smaller pieces, they created several different models using 4, 8, and 16 pieces of ice. Their math teacher saw the model and asked them what relationships they noticed between the properties of the cubes and the melting time.

Through the investigation of meaningful problems, individually or in cooperative groups, while using appropriate technology, all students...will be able to make connections linking conceptual and procedural knowledge; integrate mathematical problem-solving with other curricular areas;... [and] make connections from manipulative solutions to algorithmic solutions to technological solutions.

Delaware, Standard #4, Mathematical Connections,
Sections 4.01, 4.02, and 4.05

Mr. Eckard's Ecology Exploration

Mr. Eckard teaches an elective environmental science class to 11th and 12th graders. He wants his students to think deeply about the processes of population growth and decline. To introduce this unit, he brings his class outside and tells them the rules of Survival of the Fittest Paper Catchers (Activity 5)—students who catch their papers are able to "reproduce" by calling up other class members, while those who drop their papers "die" and must sit down. Mr. Eckard records the population size at the end of each generation. After the population size stabilizes, he adds a new rule and asks the students to predict how this rule will affect their population. When they play again, the first student drops his paper, driving the population to immediate extinction. They play once more, and after several generations the class gathers to discuss the data that Mr. Eckard recorded.

Later in the week when students complete Penny Growth (Activity 4) they talk about the strengths and limitations of the two population models. One person asks if they could replay the Paper Catchers model with the other science classes so that the population could grow larger. Several students suggest that the penny model would be more realistic if it included death. Mr. Eckard asks each student to propose a rule for penny death and predict how this rule will affect the distribution of pennies on the table as well as the size of the growing penny populations. Students present their modifications to the class and discuss how these modifications relate to mechanisms that cause death in real-world populations.

As students in grades 9–12 extend their knowledge, what they know and are able to do includes...predicting and describing the interactions of populations and ecosystems... [and] analyzing the dynamic equilibrium of ecosystems.

Colorado, Life Science, Grades 9–12, Standard 3.1

[Students should be able to] simulate and analyze factors that influence the size and stability of populations within ecosystems (e.g., birth rate, death rate, predation, migration patterns).

Illinois, Science Early High School State Goals, Section 12.B.4b

All students will...use multiple approaches to investigate and understand mathematical content... [and] apply the process of mathematical modeling to real-world problem situations.

Massachusetts, Mathematics Content, Problem Solving

Students will be able to...predict, with rationale, the effects of changing one or two factors in an ecosystem... [and] make predictions about the changes in the size or growth rate of a population; using mathematical models, e.g., from graphs and charts, students can determine relationships among the species within an ecosystem.

New Hampshire, Life Science Proficiency Standards, Curriculum Standard 3b

By the end of the 12th grade, students should know that...any mathematical model, graphic or algebraic, is limited in how well it can represent how the world works.

National Benchmarks, The Mathematical World, Symbolic Relationships, Grades 9–12

Bill's Investigation of Probability

Bill is studying probability and statistics in his 9th-grade math class. He is very proficient at solving equations but is finding it difficult to imagine the mechanisms that produce different distributions. The StarLogo project *Gaussian* resembles a Pachinko machine—balls drop from a point at the top of the screen and bounce off of a series of pins until they land in bins at the bottom of the screen. Bill plays with the project, observing the patterns of balls that result from each run.

Bill realizes that he can control the probability with which balls bounce to the right or left when they hit a pin. By changing the bias, he generates different distributions. As he develops more familiarity with the model, he begins to predict which bin will fill up the fastest. Eventually, he modifies the project so that balls drop from random places along the top of the screen. He also draws additional pins to create a rectangular pattern, in place of the original triangle. With these conditions, he is able to produce a uniform distribution. Soon he is helping other students see the relationships between the distributions that they are studying and the patterns created by his StarLogo models.

Harry's Osmosis Model

Harry is a 10th-grade biology teacher. For years he has used a "potato lab" to help his students understand osmosis and diffusion. In the potato lab, students submerge a slice of potato in distilled water and weigh the potato on successive days, noting that the potato absorbs water over time. Recently, he built a StarLogo model to enable students to visualize the molecular processes that result in the waterlogged potato.

Harry's model has a semipermeable membrane that splits the StarLogo screen in half. Water molecules start out on the right-hand side of the screen and move randomly, diffusing throughout the environment. Harry's model includes monitors that count the number of water molecules on each side of the screen. He asks his students to gather data about the amount of water on each side of the membrane at 10-second intervals. His students investigate why the number of water molecules on each half of the screen continues to fluctuate even after the water molecules appear to be in equilibrium.

When students add sugar molecules to the right-hand side of the screen, the water molecules interact with the sugar. A few students record the relative amounts of water on each side of the screen as they increase the concentration of sugar on the right-hand side. Harry encourages them to build time series plots that show how the addition of sugar molecules causes a corresponding (but not immediate) change in the distribution of water molecules.

The student is expected to... plan and implement investigative procedures including asking questions, formulating testable hypotheses, and selecting equipment and technology.

Texas, Essential Knowledge and Skills for Science, Section 112.42.c2A

[Student should know how to] investigate and identify cellular processes including homeostasis, permeability, energy production, transportation of molecules... and identify and describe the relationships between internal feedback mechanisms in the maintenance of homeostasis.

Texas, Essential Knowledge and Skills for Science, Sections 112.43.c4B and c11A

Students will... conduct scientific investigations systematically [by] using appropriate resources and technologies for research, framing the question, identifying and appropriately managing the variables, maintaining clear and accurate records... developing a practical and logical procedure, organizing, analyzing, and interpreting data, and developing conclusions based on the investigation.

Alabama, Physical Science Course, Scientific Processes, Nature of Science Content Strand

Models are simplified representations of objects, structures, or systems used in analysis, explanation, interpretation, or design. Students revise a model to create a more complete or improved representation of the system.

New York, Standard 6, Interconnectedness: Common Themes, Commencement Level, Section 2: Models

StarLogo World

This chapter describes the components of the StarLogo world. There are three main characters in the StarLogo world—turtles, patches, and the observer. The *turtles* are mobile creatures who live on a grid of patches that is arranged like a chessboard. Turtles can interact with each other and with the patches in their environment. Like real turtles, StarLogo turtles can wander around, eat food, reproduce, and die. But unlike real turtles, StarLogo turtles can also draw pictures on their environment, change colors, pile up on a single patch, and jump over dozens of patches in a single bound. When you create your own StarLogo projects, you can ask your turtles to do just about anything. The *patches* underneath the turtles are a "living" environment and can respond to commands from the turtles. In addition, the patches have a certain degree of autonomy—they can initiate some activities all by themselves.

The third character, the *observer*, watches over the StarLogo world. When the observer speaks, all of the turtles and patches listen and act accordingly. The observer also takes care of a few maintenance tasks in StarLogo, like clearing the world and creating new turtles. The observer can also create graphs and plots of turtle and patch characteristics, allowing you to think about your model in different ways. By the end of Challenge 3, you will have met all three StarLogo characters.

There are two versions of StarLogo—a universal Java-based version (called simply StarLogo) and one that is specific to Macintosh computers (called MacStarLogo). This book and this chapter both focus on the Java StarLogo version. More information on MacStarLogo can be found in Appendix A.

The information in this chapter will be most useful to you when you begin to work on StarLogo projects. You can look through this chapter now, or just remember that it is here for reference whenever you need it.

OBTAINING STARLOGO

If you don't have a copy of StarLogo, you can download it for free from **http://www.media.mit.edu/starlogo/download** or use the enclosed CD. If you are using a PC, you will need to download and install the Java version of StarLogo. If you have a Macintosh G3 or later (all iMacs and iBooks have at least a G3 processor) the Java version will run on your Mac and we strongly recommend that you use it. (If you have an older Macintosh, please see Appendix A.) On a PC, run StarLogo from the Start menu. On a Macintosh, double-click the StarLogo icon to begin using StarLogo. Once you install StarLogo, all of the sample projects and all of the projects for this book will be in folders labeled Sample Projects and Adventures Projects. You can also obtain the Adventures Projects from the CD enclosed with this book or online at **http://www.media.mit.edu/starlogo/adventures**. If you have trouble downloading StarLogo, send an email to **starlogo-request@media.mit.edu**.

About Turtles

We use *turtles* as a generic term for individuals in the StarLogo world. This usage is derived from the Logo programming language. Admittedly, *turtles* is not really generic, but we use it to describe ants, birds, and people, as well as molecules, cars, and sand.

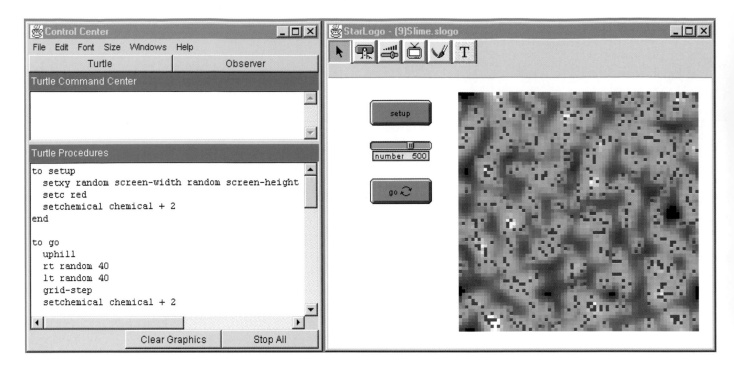

The Slime project in StarLogo.

STARLOGO IN JAVA

When you open a sample project in StarLogo, it will look something like the **Slime** project pictured above. The main elements of StarLogo are described below.

Graphics Canvas

The initially black **Graphics Canvas** of the **StarLogo Window** is a grid of patches where the turtles live. In this picture (from the **Slime** project, available in the Sample Projects folder) the turtles are red and the patches range from white to green. You can move a turtle directly by dragging it with the mouse (as long as the **Canvas** is not selected).

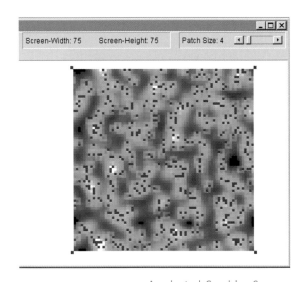

A selected Graphics Canvas.

You can change the size and shape of the **Graphics Canvas** by selecting it (press Control and click—or Shift and click on a Mac) and defining the desired shape (drag a corner handle of the **Canvas**). When the **Graphics Canvas** is selected, you can change the size of the patches using the Patch Size slider that appears in the gray border. You can also move the **Graphics Canvas** by dragging it with the mouse (just be careful not to click on a turtle and pick it up instead). The **Canvas** "wraps," meaning that if a turtle walks off the right-hand side of the screen it will reappear on the left-hand side of the screen. The same is true of the top and bottom of the **Canvas**.

Interface Window

The **Graphics Canvas** is located inside the **Interface Window**. In this window you can create interface elements like buttons, sliders, and monitors that allow you to interact directly with your StarLogo projects. Pressing a button runs that button's commands. Adjusting a slider allows you to control the value of the variable, in this case number. This **Interface** (from the *Slime* project) has two buttons and one slider. The go button is currently running, as indicated by the darker blue color.

You can add your own interface elements using the **Main Toolbar**. To learn more about buttons and sliders, see Challenges 1 and 2.

An Interface Window.

Control Center Window

The **Command Center** within the **Control Center Window** is one place that you can type StarLogo commands. These commands are run as soon as you press Return. Commands you type here can be run even if the turtles are already running other commands. If you have a StarLogo project open, enter the **Turtle Command Center** (click on the word Turtle below the menu bar if you are in the **Observer Command Center**) and try typing:

fd 5

Make sure you press Return after the command. The small black circle to the right of the command lets you know that the command is running. You can run a command again by moving the cursor back up to that line and pressing Return.

You write your own StarLogo procedures in a **Procedures Pane** of the **Control Center Window**. A procedure is a set of instructions that teaches StarLogo how to do something new. The picture shows the Turtle Procedure **setup**. You can define many procedures in your StarLogo projects. Procedures that give instructions to the turtles belong in the **Turtle Procedures Pane**, while those intended for the observer or the patches belong in the **Observer Procedures Pane**. To learn more about writing your own procedures, see Challenge 3.

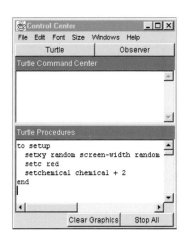

A Control Center Window.

Main Toolbar

You use the **Toolbar** to create interface elements (like buttons, sliders, and monitors) and to choose other specialized toolbars and palettes (described at the end of this chapter). For example, to create a button you would click on the button icon on the **Toolbar**. For more on creating your own interface elements, see Challenge 2.

The StarLogo Main Toolbar.

You can also look at the underlying instructions of an existing interface object. For example, if you choose the slider icon from the **Toolbar** and then click on an existing slider, you can see more about that slider. You can also inspect an interface element by choosing the arrow icon, pressing the Control key (or the Shift key on a Macintosh) and double-clicking on the element.

Plot Window

You can create real-time graphs in this window as your StarLogo project is running. For more information on how to create your own graphs and use the **Plot Window**, see Challenge 8.

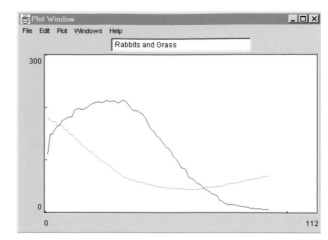

The Plot Window.

Information Window

You can put explanatory notes, commentary, and instructions in the **Information Window**. This window is also a good place to provide some background on the project you developed and teach others how to experiment with your project.

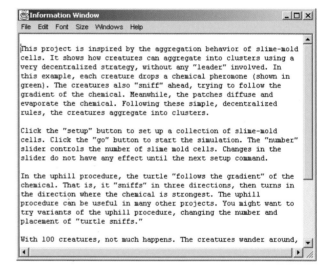

The Information Window.

Paint and Color Toolbars

The **Paint Toolbar** (on the left side of the picture) and the **Color Toolbar** (on the right side of the picture) appear when you click on the paintbrush icon in

The Paint and Color Toolbars.

the **Main Toolbar**. The **Paint Toolbar** allows you to select different types of drawing tools (like the pencil or the paintbucket) for drawing on the **Graphics Canvas**. When you paint, you can either place new turtles or simply color the patches, depending on which icon is selected (at the left of the **Color Toolbar**). With the **Color Toolbar** you can select the color that you want. The number associated with each color appears at the right of the toolbar. For instance, in this picture you can see that the square is gray, with a color number 5. For more information on color names and numbers, see **http://www.media.mit.edu/starlogo/documentation/colors.htm**. You can use the drawing tools in any project. For more information about how to use this feature of StarLogo, take a look at Challenge 2.

Activities and Challenges

The upcoming Activities and Challenges form the core of your Adventure. We suggest that, if possible, you alternate between Activities and Challenges as you proceed. This strategy will help you develop model-building skills and deepen your understanding of complex, dynamic systems.

At the beginning of each Activity and each Challenge is a list of modeling concepts covered in that exercise. Additionally, each Challenge includes descriptions of StarLogo concepts as well as definitions of particular StarLogo commands. The table on the next page describes the various conventions that we use to distinguish StarLogo commands and features. Many students find it helpful to read and refer to parts of the Challenges as they work. The Student Handouts, which are located just after the Activities and Challenges, contain concise descriptions of the Challenges and include specific StarLogo information for students. In addition, all of the StarLogo hints from the Challenges have been collected at the end of the book, in Appendix B.

ENJOY YOUR ADVENTURE!

This kind of text...	Indicates that...
setc green	You can type this command or set of commands directly into a **Command Center**, **Procedures Pane**, or button.
setc *colorname*	You should replace the italicized portion of the command with StarLogo code before typing the command in StarLogo. For instance, you could replace *colorname* with **green** or **2 * ycor**.
if *condition* [*statement*]	You should replace the italicized condition with a clause that is true or false, such as **color = green** or **energy > 5**. Then, replace the italicized statement with one or more instructions, such as **setc red** or **seth 90 jump 20**.
ask-turtles [crt 100]	You should not use these commands as they are not valid StarLogo code.
Press Control Select File Click on the go button	You should find the appropriate key, menu item, or button and press it.
Plot Window	This object is a separate window or area.
Project Title	This is a sample project that can be found in the Adventures Folder that comes on the enclosed CD.
myemail@mit.edu	This item is an email address.
http://www.mit.edu	This item is a website.
	There is a note for MacStarLogo users, which can be found in Appendix A.
	When this icon accompanies a Challenge Hint, the command is for the observer.
	When this icon accompanies a Challenge Hint, the command is for the turtles.

A Round of Applause

Sometimes, at concerts or sporting events, thousands of spectators join together in rhythmic, synchronized clapping. There is no conductor leading them. How do they coordinate their applause? Here is one way to think about what happens. Initially, when everyone starts clapping, the applause is totally unorganized. Even people clapping at the same tempo are wildly out of phase with one another. But, through some random fluctuation, a few people happen to clap at the same tempo, in phase with one another. That rhythm stands out, just a little, in the clapping noise. People in the audience sense this emerging rhythm and adjust their own clapping to join it. Thus the emerging rhythm becomes a little stronger, and even more people conform to it. Eventually, nearly everyone in the audience is clapping in a synchronized rhythm. Amazingly, the whole process takes just a few seconds, even with thousands of people participating.

Many systems in the world exhibit orderly patterns that arise in a similar manner, without any centralized control. Individuals in the systems share bits of information that help the group to achieve a level of organization, which might not have been predicted by just observing the individual interactions. Ant colonies, market economies, immune systems, and "waves" at sporting events are just a few systems in which patterns emerge from simple interactions between individuals. Participants can use this Activity as an opportunity to experience and reflect on how and why these patterns are generated.

MODELING CONCEPTS

◆ Discover how patterns can arise with no centralized control.

◆ Participate in a positive feedback loop.

◆ Explore how different ways of sensing information can influence the dynamics of a system.

MATERIALS

◆ None

RUNNING THE ACTIVITY

Ask the group to applaud and, without any further direction from you, adjust their timing until everyone is clapping in unison. Were they surprised by how much (or little) time it took for everyone to converge on the same beat? Did some people assume that it might be impossible to achieve synchronization so rapidly without a conductor? What cues did people use to synchronize their clapping? What might happen if you remove some of those cues? Ask participants to rerun the same Activity with their eyes closed. Did they converge on the same beat more or less quickly? What cues did they rely on this time?

RUNNING THE ACTIVITY—EXTENSIONS

During the first clapping game, people can rely on both auditory and visual cues to synchronize their activity. You can run a similar game that eliminates auditory cues. Ask participants to raise (and lower) their hands and adjust their timing until everyone is raising their hands in unison. How long did it take for the group to synchronize? Was this process easier or more difficult than clapping together? What does this game suggest about the use of different cues for passing information among individuals?

If you have a very talented group you might challenge them to one last synchronization game. Ask participants to form a circle, hold hands, and close their eyes. Ask them to silently squeeze each other's hands in pulses and try to synchronize the squeezes. Are they able to achieve an organized pattern? Why or why not? What cues did they use during their attempt to generate a synchronized squeeze?

FACTS FOR FACILITATORS

This Activity can be structured to take anywhere from 3 to 20 minutes. We often use it as a warm-up to some of the concepts that you will encounter during your Adventure. You can use this Activity as a starting point to help participants consider the effects of various communication strategies on a decentralized system as well as to begin a larger discussion about modeling in StarLogo.

The clapping and hand-raising games should result in fairly rapid synchronization. In fact, synchronization may happen so quickly in the clapping game that it is difficult for participants to reflect on exactly how they managed to converge on the same beat. It usually takes groups longer to sync up during the hand-raising game, providing an opportunity for participants to carefully observe the process of convergence. The squeezing game is quite difficult, and not all groups will be able to synchronize. If your group is unable to generate a synchronized squeeze, you might ask them to consider what made this third game so much harder.

To learn more about understanding decentralized systems, see Chapter 1 and Resnick (1994).

A StarLogo Modeler Is Born

Open the project *Painted Turtles.* Can you use StarLogo's turtles to create patterns? What happens to your pattern if you create only one turtle? Two turtles? Twenty turtles?

Are your favorite patterns symmetrical or asymmetrical?
Do your favorite patterns have common color schemes?
Do you prefer patterns that are dynamic or static?

Try to design your own pattern using a sequence of buttons. What happens to the pattern if you execute the steps in a different order?

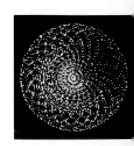

EXPLORATIONS

POSSIBLE

◆ Try varying the initial number of turtles or their starting configurations to create graphic designs using the pattern buttons. For example, click the create-flower button followed by the pattern-1 button or the pattern-2 button.

◆ Try pressing different combinations of pattern buttons or running more than one button simultaneously. Now vary these patterns by repeating them while the turtles have their pens up or down. You can further vary the patterns by resetting the turtles' colors, using the change-color button.

◆ When you feel comfortable with the above explorations, try to create some of these cool graphics for yourself.

CHALLENGE PHILOSOPHY

Using StarLogo, you can create simulations of complex systems or visualize interactions among thousands of computational creatures. But first, you'll want to become comfortable exploring and manipulating the elements of the StarLogo environment. We have discovered that *playing* with StarLogo projects is a good way to build an understanding of the modeling environment, even if this *play* might initially seem to be far removed from the models you ultimately want to build. An ounce of play now is worth a pound of effort expended later.

Challenge 1 allows you to begin to explore the nature of decentralized systems that are made up of many individuals. In particular, you should start to see that interesting and complex patterns often arise from individual actions that are based on simple rules. In addition, you should become familiar with the StarLogo interface and begin to build a basic understanding of how you can control the turtles. The concepts introduced in Challenge 1 form the foundation for the other StarLogo explorations in this book and provide a background for investigating complex systems.

StarLogo is an environment for exploration. This first Challenge is an exercise in creativity. There will be plenty of time later to learn specific commands and build models that incorporate sophisticated interactions. Now is the time to play. Like learning to speak a new language through immersion, diving into the StarLogo environment can be a great way to learn.

CHALLENGE DESCRIPTION

This Challenge demonstrates the power of parallel programming by simultaneously using many turtles to create patterns on the screen. The turtles are each programmed to follow the same rules. Yet, the patterns they create and the paths they draw can be quite complex. This Challenge uses the **Painted Turtles** project, which can be found in the Adventures Projects folder.

MODELING CONCEPTS

◆ Observe how complex behaviors and patterns can result from activating simple rules.

◆ Discover the differences between the actions of a single individual and the actions of many individuals.

◆ Explore the nature of various pattern compositions.

◆ Experiment with ways that changes in the sequence of instructions affect the final pattern.

STARLOGO CONCEPTS

◆ Use multiple turtles to draw patterns on the screen.

◆ Learn to use buttons and sliders.

◆ Understand turtle movement.

CHALLENGE GUIDELINES

Opening StarLogo

If you don't have a copy of StarLogo on your computer, see Chapter 6 for information on how to obtain your free copy. Open StarLogo and go to the File menu and Open Project... Choose the file **Painted Turtles** inside the folder called Adventures Projects. Challenge 1 uses this project as the basis for your explorations.

Painted Turtles

In the **Interface Window**, the buttons next to the **Graphics Canvas** are divided into three different categories ❶. (See the picture on the next page.) The first category is **Basic Commands** ❷. The buttons and sliders in this category perform simple StarLogo commands. The function of each button and slider is as described in the top section of the table at right.

The second category is **Setup Patterns**. The buttons and sliders in this category arrange the turtles in more complex configurations. The function of each button and slider is described in the bottom section of the table at right.

Basic Commands Buttons	Function
create number	Creates the number of turtles indicated by the slider number
forward steps	Moves each of the turtles forward the number of steps indicated by the slider steps
turn right degrees	Rotates each turtle clockwise by the number of degrees indicated by the slider degrees
clear all	Removes all graphics and kills all turtles
clear graphics	Removes all graphics
pen down	Tells all of the turtles to put their pens down
pen up	Tells all of the turtles to pick their pens up
wander (a Forever button indicated by the curved arrows to the right of "wander")	Moves and turns the turtles—like all Forever buttons, this button will stay depressed and continue running until you press it again to turn it off
change-color	Randomly changes the turtles' colors

Setup Patterns Buttons	Function
create-flower	Creates turtles in a flower shape with the number of petals indicated by the slider petals
create-2-rings	Creates two concentric circles of turtles
create-clover	Creates a clover-like shape made of turtles

The third category is **Action**. The five buttons in this category move the turtles according to collections of simple commands called procedures. You can experiment with these buttons to learn more about what they do. For example, you can try the following exploration:

❶ Press the clear all button to begin.

❷ Create 20 turtles by setting the number slider to 20 and then pressing the create number button.

❸ Put the turtles' pens down using the pen down button.

❹ Press the pattern-1 button.

Try combining the patterns from the **Action** category with some of the buttons in the **Basic Commands** category.

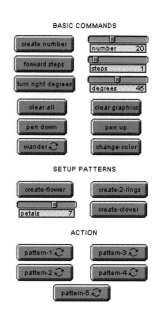

Painted Turtles' Interface.

TIPS FOR TEACHERS

Encourage your students to take advantage of the open-ended, playful nature of Challenge 1. The most important thing that they take away from Challenge 1 is a level of comfort with the StarLogo environment. Support your students as they explore the aspects of the program that are most fascinating to them (though Challenge 1 is not a good time to investigate the Turtle and Observer Procedures, as the instructions that generate the patterns include advanced commands that will be covered later). There will be many opportunities in upcoming Challenges for students to acquire specific knowledge about model building and programming. Help your students see that there are no real "mistakes" in this environment. Often, what begins as a mistake can lead to a refreshing insight or an unexpected result. Ask students to pay special attention to these opportunities for learning.

Some students may need extra support as they work through the Challenge. You may find that it is easier to guide their explorations if you have already reviewed the next Challenge. Encourage them to seek assistance first from the members of their own group and then from other classmates. Also, make sure that they save different versions of their projects as they proceed. Saved projects allow them to revert to a previous idea and to track their progress. Use the work-in-progress reports to enable students to share their insights with their classmates. Ask them to present a single idea that they learned or a particular result that they found surprising. Often, showing an early version of their project is a good way for them to describe the evolution of their idea. You can also have your students post their own Challenge solutions and discuss other students' ideas on the StarLogo Design Discussion Area (DDA) at **http://education.mit.edu/starlogo/dda**. By presenting their ideas in class and exploring other students' Challenge solutions, your students should begin to see that there is no single "right" answer to a Challenge. (See Chapter 3 for more information on work-in-progress reports and the StarLogo DDA.)

27 Blind Mice

Musicians in an orchestra take cues from the conductor as the tempo changes; students pass notes to each other during history class; football players simultaneously initiate the play as the quarterback calls "hike." In any multi-agent system, members of the system communicate with one another. Even in systems comprised of nonhuman entities, objects exchange information. For instance, billiard balls "communicate" information about their velocity and direction as they collide.

Thought of broadly, "communication" can take many forms. Sometimes communication is mediated by a central individual, like the conductor or quarterback. Other times, individual members communicate directly with one another, like the students passing notes. This Activity lets you explore the *differences between* and the *consequences of* global communication, where every group member has access to information, and local communication, where information exchange is limited to personal communication channels (which can be further constrained by the mode of communication).

27 Blind Mice is a compilation of three distinct games designed to engage participants in thinking about different types of communication strategies. In each game, the goal is the same, but the mode of information exchange that participants can use to achieve that goal is very different. In Part One, the participants usually employ centralized or global strategies, in which a small number of people take the lead and organize the others. In the latter two games, the participants' strategies shift to more decentralized or local methods, in which everyone gathers information only from people in their immediate neighborhood.

RUNNING THE ACTIVITY—PART ONE

Ask each participant to pick a random integer from 1 to 5 and write it on a Post-It note. Tell everyone to organize into like-numbered groups (i.e., all of the 1s together, all of the 2s together, and so on). Do not tell them *how* to get into their groups.

After the groups are formed, ask them to reflect on how they achieved their groupings.

- Did some people act as leaders, shouting out the numbers?

- Did others move quietly to the "correct" part of the room?

- If there were leaders, how were they chosen?

Also, look around and observe the size of the groups. Is the distribution of 1s equal to that of 2s? 3s? and so on? Is this the expected result?

RUNNING THE ACTIVITY—PART TWO

Ask participants to write a new random number on their Post-Its. Again, have everyone organize themselves into like-numbered groups—but this time, explain that they are not allowed to talk. The only way participants are allowed to communicate is by showing their Post-It notes to one another. They are not allowed to communicate in any other way: No raising fingers, no stomping feet.

MODELING CONCEPTS

- ◆ Experience the dramatic difference between local and global communication.

- ◆ Explore the process of group formation.

- ◆ Think about the effects of different ways to access information.

MATERIALS

- ◆ Post-It notes or small pieces of paper

- ◆ Pencils

- ◆ Blindfolds

When the groups have formed, ask participants to compare the two activities.

- What kinds of strategies did individuals and groups employ to find people with the same number?

- Which of these strategies was most successful?

- Are there any individuals who did not find their group? Are they alone or with others? If a small group of 3s gets together but does not ever locate the other group of 3s, a *local optimum* results because the entire group of 3s never fully convenes.

People tend to employ very different communication strategies in Game Two.

- Which game did people find easier—the one with global information or the one with more restricted, local information?

- Which game was more fun? Why?

- What kinds of systems in the natural world include strategies like those used by participants in the first game? Are there any systems that include strategies employed in the second game?

Ask participants to choose another number from 1 to 5 and write it down. The goal is the same as in the previous games: To form like-numbered groups. But this time, you will give the participants blindfolds so that they cannot see one another during the game. Explain that participants can communicate with whispers but not loud talking. Note: Make sure that people who feel uncomfortable being blindfolded do not feel obligated to participate. These people can act as monitors, making sure that other participants do not wander into dangerous situations.

When everyone has chosen a number, ask them to put on their blindfolds. When everyone is ready, have them find the people in their group. When the groups have formed (but before people remove their blindfolds), ask them to reflect on their activity.

- Did it take longer for groups to form?

- How did people feel when they found a like-numbered individual?

After they take off their blindfolds, ask them to articulate what kinds of strategies they used in this third game.

- How did their strategies differ from the first and second games?

- Are the group patterns that result from the third game different in any way from those in the first two games?

FACTS FOR FACILITATORS

Asking participants to divide into five groups works well if the total group size is between 20 and 30. If your group is significantly larger or smaller, you may want to adjust the number of different small groups accordingly.

Depending on the situation, creatures might use local or global communication strategies. StarLogo models generally incorporate behaviors that are based on local interactions. It might be helpful to think of the turtles in StarLogo as blindfolded, whispering people. Turtles are designed to react to creatures and objects in their immediate local environment. 27 Blind Mice should give participants a feel for the dramatic effects of local communication.

The 27 Blind Mice Activities were first developed by Mitchel Resnick and Uri Wilensky. For an extended description of these and other decentralized role-playing activities, see Resnick & Wilensky (1998).

Turtles, I Command Thee

Open the project **Return of the Painted Turtles**. In the **Custom Buttons** section, add your own buttons and sliders to control the turtle activity.

What kinds of patterns can you create by adding your own simple commands? What sorts of behavior can you generate using a series of commands? Can you build buttons that faithfully reproduce your favorite patterns by repeating a sequence of steps? What is the simplest set of commands you can use to create a complex pattern? Can you use the **Paint Tools** to set up different initial conditions?

EXPLORATIONS

POSSIBLE

- ◆ Try using the **repeat** command in conjunction with a slider that specifies the number of repetitions. Explore how varying the number of repetitions affects turtle behavior and the resulting pattern.

- ◆ Try to create buttons that make the turtles draw different shapes. What pattern emerges when 100 turtles each draw a triangle? You might use a slider to change the size of the shapes.

- ◆ See if you can make the turtles "wiggle" by making them repeatedly walk and turn.

Remember that StarLogo is a parallel language, so any command that you write for one turtle will be run by all of the turtles. When you issue any turtle instructions, *all* of the turtles will follow those commands.

CHALLENGE PHILOSOPHY

Well before you started building StarLogo projects, you had already created complex patterns from a set of simple rules. Remember making paper snowflakes in elementary school? When the paper was folded, you made a series of small cuts in it. When you unfolded the paper, it looked like a giant snowflake. You can think of the cuts that you made as "instructions" that you issued to the paper. Instead of appearing just once, the result of each instruction appeared many times in the final snowflake. With StarLogo you can now extend the power of parallelism to simulations that capture more complex aspects of dynamic systems.

In the last Challenge, you saw turtles following simple rules and creating complex patterns. In this Challenge, you will learn more about how to create your own rules for individual creatures. You can continue to investigate how those rules translate into observable patterns when many individuals execute them at the same time.

Using StarLogo models, such as the one you experimented with in Challenge 1, is a good way to become familiar with the StarLogo environment. You will enjoy an even greater sense of excitement and accomplishment when you take more control of the turtles by programming your own rules. Perhaps you already started opening up the buttons during Challenge 1. If so, this Challenge provides some structure, and ample opportunity, to continue that exploration. If not, this Challenge is a good chance to begin investigating how buttons work. Either way, this Challenge is designed to help everyone begin learning the StarLogo language.

Challenge 2 also introduces the **Paint Tools**. You may find that you want to spend extra time painting with turtles and patches and then watching what happens when you run simple commands from a variety of starting conditions. This kind of play is informative, as many complex systems exhibit different dynamics if you slightly alter the starting conditions. These explorations can also be quite addicting, even for those of us who have used StarLogo for years! If you get intrigued by this exploration, you might check out an Active Essay at **http://el.www.media.mit.edu/groups/el/projects/emergence**. This Active Essay is a web-based cellular automata (patches only) game that explores how different starting conditions can result in vastly different patterns.

In this Challenge, you will build on the last project, **_Painted Turtles_**, by adding your own buttons and sliders to control the turtles in new ways. You can also change the environment (or set up a unique pattern of turtles) using the **Paint Tools**. Starting with a simple set of commands, you can learn the power of making small changes in a parallel language, since any small change is run simultaneously by every turtle. Be assured that the StarLogo language is quite rich, but don't get bogged down trying to learn every command. Now is a good time to explore the subtlety and diversity that can be created with a few basic commands. Just as a

MODELING CONCEPTS

◆ Design individual-based action sequences.

◆ Experiment with simple rules to create complex behaviors.

◆ Explore the ways in which small changes in a rule can produce dramatic changes in the resulting pattern.

STARLOGO CONCEPTS

◆ Create buttons to run simple StarLogo commands and call more complex procedures.

◆ Learn how to create slider variables and watch how they can influence turtle processes.

◆ Distinguish between once and **Forever** buttons.

◆ Create new features in the environment using the **Paint Tools**.

novice athlete can make more rapid progress by focusing on mastering the basics of her sport, your progress will be bolstered if you initially concentrate on fully mastering a basic set of commands.

CHALLENGE DESCRIPTION

In Challenge 2, you will be using a variation of the project that you used in the last Challenge. However, when you open up *Return of the Painted Turtles*, you will see a section at the bottom labeled CUSTOM BUTTONS 🍎. In this area you will be adding your own buttons to control the turtles. You are also free to explore and change the existing buttons. Try using the **Paint Tools** to add turtles and patches that create new patterns. The *Return of the Painted Turtles* project can be found in the Adventures Projects folder.

CHALLENGE GUIDELINES

There are several key ideas that you will encounter in the process of tackling this Challenge. You will learn to create your own interface elements (in this case, buttons and sliders).

Creating Buttons

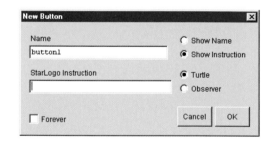

A button editor.

To create a new button:

❶ Click on the blue button icon in the **Toolbar**.

❷ In the **Interface** area, click and hold where you want to place the button. Drag the mouse down and to the right until you get to where you want to place the lower right-hand corner (you will see a rectangle the size of your new button). Release the mouse button.

❸ A button editor for the new button will pop up 🍎. Fill out the information for your button. If you'd like, you can name the button and click in the Show Name radio button. If you want the button to operate continuously, you should click the Forever check box. Finally, you should add the commands that you want the button to execute by typing them into the StarLogo Instruction field (you can type many commands in a row within a single button). Be sure that you check whether the StarLogo Instructions are for the turtles or the observer. Refer to the hints below for more information on specific actions that you can program into your buttons and the difference between Turtle and Observer Commands 🍎.

❹ Click OK.

You may also want to perform some of the button operations on the next page.

Action	Process
Modify the contents of a button	Click the button icon on the **Main Toolbar**. Next, click on the button you want to change. Inside the button editor, you can change the button name and instructions, decide whether to show the name or instructions, mark whether the instructions are for the turtles or the observer, and choose if the button should run continuously (check Forever).
Delete a button	Press Control (or Shift on a Macintosh) and click on the button once, so that the little square handles appear. Press the Delete key.
Resize a button	Press Control (or Shift on a Macintosh) and click on the button once, so that the little square handles appear. To resize the button, click and hold the mouse button down while dragging one of the handles until the button is the desired size.
Move a button	Press Control (or Shift on a Macintosh) and click on the button once, so that the little square handles appear. Drag the button to the desired location.

As mentioned in Step 3 above, in order for the button to do something you will need to enter some commands in the StarLogo Instruction field of the button editor. The following hints will help you get started. Try using the commands in your buttons .

If you want to...	Use these commands:	For this character:
Create turtles	The command **crt** *number* creates the number of turtles specified by *number*. Turtles are created in the center of the screen. Experiment with creating one or more turtles to discover their colors and headings.	
Move turtles	The command **fd** *step* moves each turtle forward the number of steps specified by *step*. Try: **fd 4**. Watch what happens when a turtle walks off the edge of the screen. The command **bk** *step* moves each turtle back the specified number of steps (but doesn't turn the turtle around).	

(Challenge Hints continue on the next page)

If you want to...	Use these commands:	For this character:
Change turtle direction	Turtle direction can be changed in several ways. One way is to rotate all of the turtles some number of degrees using the command **rt** *angle* where *angle* is the number of degrees you want the turtles to rotate clockwise. Try: **rt 45**. You can use **lt** *angle* in the same way. You can also set all turtles to the same heading using the command **seth** *direction* where *direction* is the heading on a compass (0 is towards the top of the screen) that you want the turtles facing. Try: **seth 45**.	
Change turtle color	Turtle color can be changed with the **setc** *newcolor* command, which changes all of the turtles to the color specified by *newcolor*. Note that *newcolor* can be simple color names (e.g., **red** or **blue**) or any number from 0 to 139. Try: **setc 105** or **setc blue**.	
Have turtles draw paths	Each turtle has a pen that can be in the up or down position. You can control this using the **pu** (**pen up**) and **pd** (**pen down**) commands. If a turtle's pen is down, it leaves a trail wherever it goes.	
Repeat a given statement multiple times	The statement **repeat** *times* [*statements*] will repeat the *statements* inside the square brackets the number of *times* you specify. For example, if you wanted a turtle to move forward 10 steps and turn right 30 degrees 5 times in a row you would use the statement: repeat 5 [fd 10 rt 30]	 depending on which one is able to execute *statements*
Clear all of the turtles and patches	The command **ca** removes all of the turtles and resets the patches to black.	
Remove all turtles from the world	The command **ct** kills all turtles but leaves the patches alone.	
Turn all of the patches black	The command **cg** clears the **Graphics Canvas**, by resetting all of the patches to black, but does not kill the turtles.	

CHALLENGE HINTS

If you explore some of the pattern buttons in ***Return of the Painted Turtles***, you will notice that they do not use the statements given above but instead say things like go1 or setup2. These are *procedures* (several commands strung together and associated with a name) that have been written by another StarLogo user and are contained in the **Procedures Panes**. In the next Challenge, you will be writing your own procedures.

Distinguishing Between Turtle and Observer Commands

You might be wondering why you always need to specify whether the commands in your buttons are designated for the turtles or the observer. StarLogo needs to know which characters are supposed to run the commands you type. So any time you make a new button or write a new command or procedure, you need to think about which character you want to run those commands and then tell StarLogo. In the StarLogo documentation each command indicates whether it can be run by the turtles or the observer (<u>http://www.media.mit.edu/starlogo/documentation</u>) 🍎.

Creating Sliders

As you experiment with some of the buttons, you may notice that you are trying to find just the right value for the number of steps you want the turtles to walk forward or the number of degrees you want them to turn. Instead of retyping the values each time, you can use sliders to change these values.

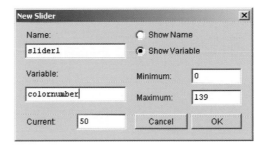

A slider editor.

There are three steps to using a slider: Creating a new slider, naming the slider, and then using the slider name instead of a number inside the button. This process is most easily illustrated in an example. The following steps create a slider that specifies the color of all of the turtles and a button that changes their color:

❶ Create a new slider by going to the **Toolbar** and clicking on the green slider icon.

❷ Click and drag in the **Interface** area where you want the slider to go.

❸ A slider editor for the new slider will pop up 🍎. Type the name colornumber in the space called Variable, and enter 0 as the minimum value, 139 as the maximum value, and 50 as the current value.

❹ Click OK.

Now that you know how to make buttons and sliders try creating a new button and giving it the Turtle Command setc colornumber. In order to try your button, you will need to create some turtles. Make another button with the Observer Command crt 50 (only the observer can create new turtles from scratch). Then select a value on your slider and click the buttons you created. What would happen if you also made a button that moved your turtles forward? What would happen if you turned the setc colornumber button into a Forever button?

Paint Tools

One more StarLogo feature introduced in Challenge 2 is the **Paint Tools**. You have already seen that you can create turtles using the Observer Command **crt** *number* (which creates as many turtles as you specify) and you can color the patches using the **pd** command (which paints the patches as the turtles walk on them). Additionally, you can create turtles and color patches using the **Paint Tools.** To enter the painting mode and get to the **Paint Tools**, click on the paintbrush icon in the **Main Toolbar.**

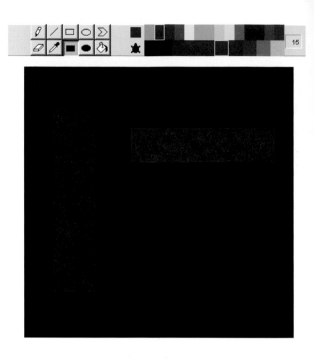

The Paint and Color Toolbars and the Graphics Canvas.

Once you are in painting mode, you can paint the patches by choosing the color you want from the Color palette (the chosen color will appear in the square above the turtle in the picture) and then clicking on a paint tool like the pencil or the paint bucket . As you paint with these tools on the **Graphics Canvas**, you will be coloring the underlying patches.

If, instead of patches, you would like to add new turtles to your StarLogo project, click on the turtle just under the colored square. Now when you choose a painting tool like the pencil or the paint bucket, you will be painting new turtles into your project! If you type **fd 1** in the **Turtle Command Center**, all of those new turtles will move. You can exit paint mode by clicking on the arrow tool. If you want to move a turtle by hand, then click on it and drag it around by holding the mouse button down (make sure that you have the arrow selected, not the paintbrush). Remember, however, that you won't be able to drag the patches because they are not mobile.

TIPS FOR TEACHERS

Even though Challenge 2 is shorter than many of the other Challenges, it introduces some important concepts including creating buttons, integrating sliders, and modifying a project using the **Paint Tools**. While you might allocate less time to this Challenge, we strongly suggest that you do not skip over it. If absolutely necessary, it is better to combine Challenges 1 and 2 than to omit Challenge 2.

At this point, students should be comfortable with a number of basic StarLogo concepts, including differentiating between Turtle and Observer Commands, creating functional buttons and sliders, and programming simple commands. Students should recognize that when they write a Turtle Command once, all of the turtles in the project run that command. While their understanding of parallelism won't be complete, they should begin to exhibit a sense of its power. For instance, a student might discover that creating a hundred turtles and asking them to move forward 10 steps forms a circle. As in Challenge 1, it is not important that students understand the code in the Turtle and Observer Procedures (such as **go1** and **setup3**) as those procedures use complex commands that are covered later in the book.

When students are deciding whether to use **rt/lt** or **seth**, it might be helpful for them to think of how they give someone directions. When the person needs to make a turn, they can tell her to make a right-hand turn (which is affected by the direction she is currently facing) or they can tell her to take the road to the north (which is independent of the direction she is facing). Ask them to experiment with these two methods.

During the work-in-progress reports, you can ask students how they came up with their design ideas, as well as how they programmed them. You can also ask them to describe their most difficult StarLogo bug or the most surprising result they obtained. These whole group meetings can be a good opportunity for students to ask each other how they achieved their solutions.

You can expect students to demonstrate a wide range of proficiency in their responses to Challenge 2. Some students will stick to using single commands, while others will be anxious to begin writing procedures. Encourage the first group to experiment with putting multiple commands in a single button. You might also suggest that they ask a classmate for some assistance. Challenge the second group to create the most intricate pattern with the fewest number of commands. You might also encourage them to explore some of the sample projects that come with StarLogo. We often shuffle groups after every Challenge to give students an opportunity to work with other people and to make sure that groups are composed of students with a diverse set of talents.

Pixelated Paths

Learning how to build a StarLogo model requires learning how to translate an initial image of what the turtles should do into a precise description of how they should do it. In this Activity, participants start by drawing a path, then develop a description to help others recreate the path without ever seeing it. We suggest that this Activity take place just before Challenge 3.

RUNNING THE ACTIVITY

Give participants a sheet of graph paper and ask that each of them draw a path on the paper. The path should consist of a series of straight lines, connected at right angles. It will be easier for participants to complete the next step of the Activity if they draw lines in the middle of the squares on the graph paper, instead of on top of the preprinted lines. They should also indicate the beginning of the path (with a turtle pointing in the starting direction of the path) and the end of the path.

Next, each participant will create a set of "landmarks" to help someone else re-create the path, without ever seeing it. Have participants place tracing paper on top of their graph paper, and mark the starting position and direction of the turtle on the tracing paper. Then participants should create colored landmarks on the tracing paper, telling the turtle where to go according to following the rules:

❶ If you see a red square,
   then turn all the way around (180°).

❷ If you see a green square,
   then turn left (90°).

❸ If you see a blue square,
   then turn right (90°).

The goal is to place enough landmarks so that the turtle will follow the entire path from beginning to end.

Have each person exchange tracing paper (not the original path) with a partner. Each partner should follow the landmarks indicated on the tracing paper and draw the turtle's path directly on the tracing paper, without consulting the author or the original path. The turtle should begin walking straight ahead from the starting point, turning whenever it bumps into a landmark. The goal is for the turtle to reach the end of the path just by following the rules.

When all participants have finished, ask them to compare the tracing paper paths with the originals.

- How many people were able to accurately follow their partner's path?

- Were there any silly mistakes? (Did some people forget certain color blocks or use the wrong colors?)

- What strategies resulted in the most successful path followings? (Larger color blocks, simpler paths, predictable patterns?)

- What would happen if people drew curvy paths? What other rules would make it easier to follow these paths?

FACTS FOR FACILITATORS

The turtles in StarLogo are not very smart on their own. When giving the turtles instructions (writing procedures or commands) it is important to specify exactly what you want them to do. You should include instructions like where you want them to begin, which direction they should be heading, what you want them to do at a certain point, and so forth.

Many students are surprised at the degree of specificity required to make the turtles behave in the ways that they imagine. Turtles have no "intuition" to figure out what students mean by partially completed instructions. Just like incomplete diagrams in this Activity, incomplete instructions will not enable the turtles to accomplish the task that students are intending. You can use this Activity to help students appreciate the need for including explicit detail in their StarLogo projects.

MODELING CONCEPTS

◆ Use simple rules to control sophisticated behaviors.

◆ Learn about the level of detail required to have turtles accurately follow instructions.

◆ Practice giving instructions that turtles can understand.

MATERIALS

◆ Graph paper

◆ Tracing paper

◆ Red, green, blue, and black markers

Landmark Decisions

Can you make your turtles react to obstacles in their environment? Perhaps you can make your turtles walk along a path that you create, such as the one shown below, by drawing obstacles that guide the turtles.

You can paint colors in the turtles' environment and then use the following procedure to make the turtles react to the colors as they move:

```
to check-patches
  if pc-ahead = red [rt 180]
  if pc-ahead = green [lt 90]
  if pc-ahead = blue [rt 90]
end
```

Try building a StarLogo project that has turtles walking on a particular path or reacting to obstacles in the environment in a meaningful way. Be sure to put the **check-patches** procedure in the **Turtle Procedures Pane 🍎 8**. If you want to see an example that uses these commands, check out the *Bumper Turtles* project in the Adventures Projects folder.

EXPLORATIONS

POSSIBLE

◆ As you are drawing obstacles on the screen, consider whether you want the obstacles to take up a lot or a little of the screen.

◆ Try making slight alterations to the location of your obstacles. How do these modifications affect the paths that the turtles follow?

◆ Experiment with different path widths and vary the number of turtles simultaneously walking on the path. When you create multiple turtles, do all of them walk the same way?

◆ Try adding a small amount of randomness to each step as the turtles walk.

◆ Think about real-world metaphors for the **check-patches** procedure. What do they suggest about how you might program the turtles or build the obstacles?

CHALLENGE PHILOSOPHY

What does a pinball bouncing off of bumpers have in common with a bee using landmarks to navigate back home from a flower patch? Both of these examples are instances of individuals reacting to other objects in their environment. When bees fly back to the hive they depend on landmarks in the environment to reach their destination. A bee might remember to turn left at the large oak tree and fly straight until reaching the creek, where one last right turn will bring her to the hive. Any change in the spatial arrangement of the landmarks can be devastating for the bees. If someone cuts down the large oak tree, then the bees will be unable to react to that landmark and may never reach the hive. Just as the arrangement of the landmarks is important for the bees, the location of the bumpers influences the pinball's path. In both examples, the spatial arrangement of the obstacles affects the behavior of the individuals.

This Challenge introduces the concept of individuals reacting to their environment. Unlike many other modeling tools, StarLogo enables you to create a system with a spatially meaningful environment in which you can see how the individuals that you create react to their surroundings.

This Challenge provides a perfect opportunity to get comfortable with the two main characters in the StarLogo world—turtles and patches. Turtles are mobile creatures that run around on the **Graphics Canvas**, while patches are stationary "environmental" objects that cover the entire **Graphics Canvas** in a grid. You can usually see the turtles as they move around the screen, but you might have missed the patches. There are, however, patches covering the **Graphics Canvas** in every StarLogo project .

In this Challenge, you will work with turtles and patches and begin to explore the interactions between them. Unlike the first two Challenges, you will be writing your own code now. Writing procedures might be a new experience if you have been controlling the turtles primarily through the use of buttons and sliders. It is easy to get started on procedure writing if you write short procedures and test them each time you add a new instruction. This process allows you to see the effects of the change that you just made, and lets you make sure that things are working before you make so many changes that you are unable to backtrack in case of a mistake. You can also try out individual commands in the **Command Centers** before inserting them into your procedures. These techniques will make the debugging process much more efficient!

MODELING CONCEPTS

- Differentiate between individuals and their environment.

- Discover how the environment can change the actions of individuals.

- Construct simple rules to control how individuals react to their environment.

- Explore the influence of spatial structure in a model.

STARLOGO CONCEPTS

- Create a new project using both turtles and patches.

- Use Turtle Procedures and patches to control the movement of turtles.

- Understand that all of the turtles run the same instructions simultaneously in StarLogo.

CHALLENGE DESCRIPTION

Challenge 3 asks you to build a model in which turtles react to obstacles in their environment. This interaction is based on a simple rule that enables the turtles to check the color of the patch one step ahead of them and turn different directions based on that color. Using the **Paint Tools**, you will design and construct obstacles in the environment and investigate how different arrangements of these obstacles affect turtle behavior.

There are many ways to imagine and program interactions between turtles and patches. This Challenge introduces one method—the **check-patches** procedure. As you experiment, you might think of other methods or procedures that would describe or facilitate different interactions.

This Challenge works best when it is immediately preceded by Pixilated Paths (Activity 3). That Activity helps illustrate just how specific you will need to be when giving instructions to the turtles and how one minor mistake can result in a vastly different pattern (though sometimes these patterns can be more interesting than the one that you intended to create).

CHALLENGE GUIDELINES

Starting a New Project

In Challenge 3, you will start your own new project and begin writing procedures. First, you need to create a new StarLogo project. Go to the File menu in the **Control Center** menu bar and select New 🍎. (You may need to answer a question about saving a previous project, if you haven't already saved your work.) The first time that you launch the StarLogo application, there are some turtles sitting in the middle of the screen, but when you make a new file, you will have to create your own turtles.

Separating Turtle and Observer Commands

In the last Challenge, you learned how to differentiate Turtle and Observer Commands. A Forever button that instructed **fd 1 rt random 3** had to be identified as a Turtle button, while a button that instructed **ca crt 15** was identified as an Observer button. Similarly, when you use the **Command Centers** and **Procedures Panes** you will first need to select Turtle or Observer modes by clicking on the appropriate button in the **Control Center** 🍎. Notice that in Turtle mode the **Control Center** has a green header, while in Observer mode the header is brown. These colors correspond to colors in the documentation that identify commands as Turtle or Observer Commands.

If you try to issue a command to the wrong character, then you will get an error that says something like "turtle can't call a primitive observer command crt." If you are unsure of where a command belongs, then think about which character you would like to run the command or check in the documentation. Some commands can be run by both the turtles and the observer, often with different results. Try typing **show pc-at 0 0** in the two **Command Centers**. The observer reports the value of the patch color at the center of the screen. Each turtle reports the value of the patch color that is underneath it.

It is sometimes convenient, especially when setting the initial conditions of your project, to have the observer set up the turtles. Use the **ask-turtles** command in Observer mode to accomplish this goal. For example, try: **crt 10 ask-turtles [fd random 60]**. Alternatively, you can set up the initial conditions using the **Paint Tools**.

Command Centers

Start by typing some commands in the two **Command Centers**. Play around with moving your turtles, changing their colors, clearing the screen, and creating additional turtles. The **Command Centers** are good places to test new commands. To run commands, just type them and press Return. You can put many commands in a **Command Center**. If you put more than one command on a single line, then all of the commands on that line will be run when you press Return. When you are comfortable running both Turtle and Observer Commands, then you can begin writing procedures.

Procedures

In this Challenge, you will encounter procedures, possibly for the first time. Procedures are just combinations of commands that tell StarLogo how to execute compound actions. You can think about new procedures as ways to teach StarLogo new words. Every time you write a new procedure, you are "teaching" StarLogo a new word. You convey this to StarLogo by starting procedures with the word **to** and finishing with the word **end** as in the Turtle Procedure **to dance** (see chart at right).

to dance	In English this reads:
fd 10	move forward ten steps
wait 1	wait one second
bk 2	move back two steps
wait 1	wait one second
rt 75	turn right 75 degrees
fd 3	move forward three steps
end	

Everything between **to dance** and **end** tells StarLogo what you mean when you call the procedure **dance**. Notice that this procedure is designed for turtles, which means that you should write it in the **Turtle Procedures Pane**. Notice also that this procedure assumes that you already have turtles 🐢. If you don't have any, then use the **crt** command in the **Observer Command Center** to create some. Now try typing the

dance procedure in the **Turtle Procedures Pane** and then typing **dance** in the **Turtle Command Center**. What happens if you make a Forever button with **dance** as the instruction?

In StarLogo, procedure names can only be a single word long. Also, you can teach an old dog new tricks (by writing new procedures), but you cannot teach an old dog something he already knows. In other words, make sure you do not try to name procedures "turtle," "patch," "color," or other words already contained in the StarLogo language. StarLogo already understands these words and will not accept any new definitions.

The core of this Challenge is a short procedure that the turtles use to turn in different directions depending on the color of the patch that they "see" in front of them. This procedure is a Turtle Procedure because it is the turtles who are individually checking the patches directly in front of them.

	In English this reads:

to check-patches
    if pc-ahead = red [rt 180]
 	
    if pc-ahead = green [lt 90]
 	
    if pc-ahead = blue [rt 90]
end
	
	if the patch color one step ahead of me is
	    red, then turn around
	if the patch color one step ahead of me is
	    green, then turn left
	if the patch color one step ahead of me is
	    blue, then turn right

Once you have written this procedure, you can just type **check-patches** in the **Turtle Command Center**. The turtles will understand what you mean and will execute those three commands. Of course, if you open a new project in which you want to use the **check-patches** procedure, you will need to enter it again in the **Turtle Procedures Pane**. Just remember that the **check-patches** procedure doesn't ask the turtles to move anywhere, so right now they will just check the color and turn. If you want them to move, you will have to add another line to your procedure that tells them to move forward a certain number of steps (such as **fd 1**). Once you have written a procedure, you can call it from the appropriate **Command Center**, a button, or within another procedure.

The following three projects are examples that use the **check-patches** and other similar procedures. You may elect to go directly to the Challenge to create your own project and later return to these samples for additional inspiration. Alternatively, you can start exploring them now to gain a better understanding of different ways to use this procedure before building your own project.

Bumper Turtles

In this project, the turtles change direction every time they bounce off of an "obstacle." Depending on the color of the obstacle, the turtle will turn either to the right, to the left, or all the way around.

Click the setup button to set up the turtle in its initial position. Then click the go button to start the simulation. If you want to try adding some randomness to the turtle's path, stop the go button and then press the go and wiggle button.

The Bumper Turtles' Graphics Canvas.

By using the pen-down and pen-up buttons, you can control whether or not the turtle marks the path that it follows by drawing on the patches with its pen. To erase the turtle's path use clear-path, which clears only the yellow path drawn by the turtle.

As you are exploring this project, try using the clear-graphics button and then drawing your own obstacles. You can do this by using the **Paint Tools** as described in Challenge 2. Just remember that in the **check-patches** procedure, the turtles only look for red, green, and blue obstacles (colors 15, 55, and 105 respectively). Consider what this project would look like with many turtles instead of only one turtle. You can study this by changing the value of the number slider. Also, notice that in this project two of the lines of code in **check-patches** call **check-patches** again. Can you figure out why the code asks the turtles to look in front of them twice? Try removing those two calls to see what happens. Now can you figure it out?

The Interface from Bumper Turtles.

Follow the Leader

This project starts off like **Bumper Turtles** with a turtle checking patch color and turning accordingly. The first turtle in this project, however, draws with its pen down, leaving a path behind it. When a second turtle is created, it begins in a slightly different location than the first turtle. Notice that when this turtle starts moving it winds up following the path of the first turtle. This demonstrates a simple way that the first turtle can influence the environment and subsequently affect the behavior of another turtle. You will explore this idea more extensively in Challenge 4.

To use this project, click on the setup first turtle button. Then click the go button to see the first turtle draw its path. Now, click setup second turtle and then go and watch what happens. Try clicking the setup second turtle button and pressing go several times. What happens if you press the clear button and then setup the second turtle?

The Interface from Follow the Leader.

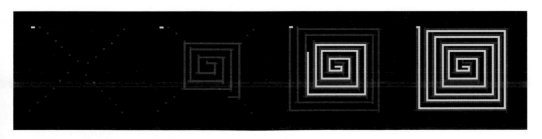

Follow the Leader's Graphics Canvas over time.

Yellow Brick Road

This project introduces a real-world metaphor for the **check-patches** procedure. The creators of this project changed **check-patches** to **check-color**. As the turtles (or "cars" in this model) **check-color**, they adjust their speeds according to the color of the patch ahead of them. The car speeds are controlled using the sliders car1_speed and car2_speed. Notice that only one car pays attention to the Red_Zone.

By adjusting the sliders, you can manipulate the speed of the cars on the track. What would this project look like if there were many more cars? How could you change the project to include intersections? Can you think of a way to let the cars choose whether to turn right or left? The following commands may be useful as you proceed 🍎.

CHALLENGE HINTS

If you want to...	Use these commands:	For this character:
Find out the patch color of the patch that a turtle is sitting on	The command **pc** returns the color of the patch that a turtle is on.	
Get the color of the patch directly in front of a turtle	The command **pc-ahead** returns the color of the patch directly in front of a turtle 🍎.	
Find out the patch color of a specific patch	The command **pc-at** *x-coordinate y-coordinate* returns the patch color of that individual patch, relative to the character's position (the observer always "sits" at 0 0 while the turtles can be anywhere). Try typing **show pc-at 1 1** in both the **Turtle** and **Observer Command Centers** and see what happens.	
Generate a random number	The command **random** *number* will generate a random number from 0 to *number* – 1. For example, **random 3** will return 0, 1, or 2.	
Do something only if a certain condition is satisfied	The conditional **if** *condition* [*statement*] will execute *statement* if the stated *condition* is true. For example, the statement **if (pc = red) [rt 90]** will cause all turtles on red patches to turn 90 degrees to the right.	depending on whether Turtle or Observer Commands make up the *statement*

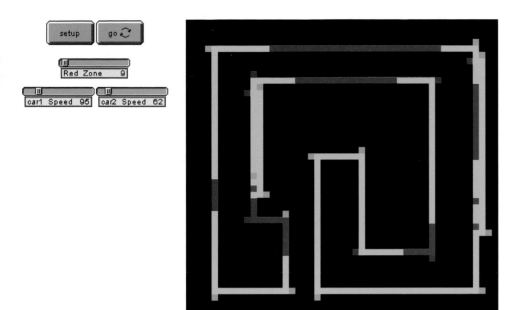

TIPS FOR TEACHERS

We highly recommend that you run Pixilated Paths (Activity 3) just prior to Challenge 3. That Activity was designed to help students understand how simple rules can mediate interactions between creatures and their environment. It also highlights the importance of specificity when programming turtles and coloring patches.

By the end of Challenge 3, students should be comfortable with the three main StarLogo characters—turtles, patches, and the observer—and the difference between Turtle and Observer Commands. If students are having trouble visualizing the difference between turtles and patches, encourage them to open the project *Big Bumper Turtles*. In this project, the patch size (and therefore the turtle size too) is larger. All of the obstacles are only a single patch big, and the turtles walk only in the cardinal compass directions. Have students explore this project with the yellow turtles' pens up and down. *Big Bumper Turtles* also eliminates the need to call the **check-patches** procedure twice, since the size and spacing of the obstacles and the direction of the turtles' paths guarantee that once a turtle has turned away from an obstacle its path is clear.

While some students will be eager to create their own projects, others might be more hesitant. At this stage, there is no need for all students to begin their projects from scratch. They should feel comfortable modifying sample projects. Encourage all of your students to try their ideas without worrying about making mistakes. Debugging is an important part of the learning process. As students make new discoveries or get stuck on particular implementations, encourage them to discuss their projects with their classmates. This cross-fertilization helps students make progress on their own work and creates a classroom dynamic that supports optimal use of your time.

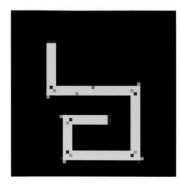

The Graphics Canvas from Tortoise Hare.

Challenge 3 is a turning point in your Adventure. In the first two Challenges, students were making only small modifications to existing projects. Now that students are becoming proficient in StarLogo, they will be able to incorporate more of their own ideas into their Challenge solutions. That opens new learning opportunities for your students, but it can make it more difficult for you to anticipate (and critique) what your students will produce. In order to give you a sense of what you can expect, some of the projects in the Adventures Projects folder are actual student solutions. For example, *Follow the Leader*, *Yellow Brick Road*, and *Tortoise Hare* were all created by students. Clearly, not every solution will be as polished as the ones we chose to include. While you should expect a great diversity of Challenge solutions, you can gauge your students' work based partially upon the sample projects that we provide.

As students' projects become more complex, the work-in-progress reports have a tendency to run too long. Students often exhaustively describe every aspect of their projects. You may be pleased with their enthusiasm, but in all likelihood you will need to help them focus their presentations. Encourage them to highlight just one aspect of their project. If they are still unfocused, you might ask them to write down their topic before describing their group's project to the class. Alternatively, you can use the StarLogo DDA as a way to structure their reports (**http://education.mit.edu/starlogo/dda**). With other students, you may have to prompt them to describe their projects. In our experience this kind of questioning is quite different from many other classroom interactions. We suggest that you prepare a few questions about the Challenge that students can answer meaningfully and briefly. For instance, find out if the group was able to achieve the look and feel of the interactions that they wanted. If not, what would they try next? Or ask them if they modified **check-patches**, and if so, what their modification accomplished. Or encourage them to predict what would happen to their projects if they added many more turtles or instructed the turtles to draw paths as they moved.

Beginning to explore the ways that creatures can interact with their environment is quite exciting. Many students will be able to imagine interesting and complex projects. At this point, it is important to help them limit the scope of their projects, remembering that they have just started on their StarLogo Adventure. The upcoming Challenges offer further opportunities to build on the ideas that they have now. You may want to look ahead so that you can help them select aspects of their ideas that are appropriate for each Challenge.

Watch Your Investments Grow

Did you ever count bacterial colonies growing in a petri dish? Or track the accumulation of money in your savings account? Or watch as mold spread over an old piece of bread? If so, you have observed population growth in action. As populations grow, the change in the number of individuals in those populations over time can be classified in different ways. Exponential growth and logistic growth are terms applied to specific patterns of population expansion. Both exponential and logistic growth are central to many processes and are the basis for many models. Perhaps because of their prevalence, or perhaps because of their "observable" quality, these types of growth are commonly described in biology, mathematics, and even economics courses. However, most textbooks present them in terms of somewhat sophisticated mathematical equations. Unfortunately, those equations do not provide a handy structure for thinking about growing systems from the "bottom up."

In this Activity, you will get a chance to explore exponential and logistic growth models, relying on simple rules and observable aggregate behavior rather than on specialized mathematical techniques. This Activity approaches system modeling from the perspective of one individual or one creature—much like StarLogo does. The penny model presented in this Activity is an *idea model*. You might think about the advantages and limitations that this type of model provides for understanding exponential and logistic growth. You might also consider what modifications would be required to create a penny-based *minimal model for a system*.

MODELING CONCEPTS

◆ Discover how simple rules can define behavior that is typically described by complex mathematical equations.

◆ Learn about the concepts of exponential and logistic growth.

◆ Analyze the elements of a model that make it appropriate or inappropriate for thinking about specific systems.

MATERIALS

◆ String

◆ Approximately 250 pennies per group

◆ Note paper and graph paper

RUNNING THE ACTIVITY

In this Activity, each group will "grow" a population of pennies. Start by dividing the participants into three or more small groups. Give one group a small piece of string (about a foot long), another group a medium-sized piece of string (about two feet long), and the final group a long piece of string (a few feet long). If you have more than three groups, you can give out varying string lengths or give two groups the same string length. Have each group form their string into a circle on a large flat surface. Give each group three pennies and have them place the pennies "randomly" inside the string circle. Then distribute the rest of the pennies. Explain the following rules:

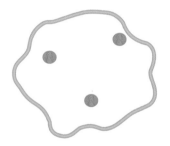

❶ The pennies must all lie flat on the surface of the table (or floor).

❷ Pennies can only "live" inside the string circle.

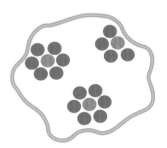

❸ Every time step, reproduction is simulated by placing the maximum number of "offspring" pennies around the perimeter of every "parent" penny.

❹ Pennies reproduce synchronously. This process means that a generation happens in a single time step, during which every "parent" penny reproduces to the full extent that it can.

Ask each group to begin penny reproduction and to note the number of pennies at the end of each generation. Groups can record either the total number of pennies or the number of new offspring pennies. Later you might discuss the relationship between these two measures. Let each group proceed at its own pace. Groups with shorter strings usually finish before the other groups. As groups finish, ask them to graph the numbers of pennies over time. After some time, stop the remaining groups and have them construct the same graphs.

Compare all of the graphs. Most likely the short-string graphs will illustrate logistic (S-shaped) growth, while the long-string graphs will show exponential (continually accelerating) growth. Ask the groups to discuss the following issues:

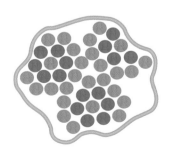

Three generations of penny growth. The first generation is shown in red, the second in blue, and the third in green.

- What effect does the length of string have on the population growth?

- What effect does the initial placement of pennies have? Very few groups will actually place their pennies in truly random initial positions, so you may want to compare groups' methods for placing their pennies.

- Are there some animals whose growth might resemble the penny growth? If so, do all of the graphs represent growth patterns of the same animals?

- Would these models be appropriate ways to describe a gazelle population on the open plains of Africa? How about fish in a pond? Why or why not?

- What kinds of modifications might enable this model to better represent other systems?

Consider running the model again with one or more of the following modifications:

- Have the pennies move around after each generation is done reproducing.

- Invent a mechanism for simulating sexual reproduction (e.g., require two pennies to be less than an inch apart for them to give birth to a new penny).

- Add ways for the pennies to die. This alteration might be a random method that selects a few pennies to die each generation or it might be a predictable mechanism, such as one that causes pennies in crowded areas to die.

Do those modifications change the answers to some of the questions above?

FACTS FOR FACILITATORS

Encourage participants to think of ways that this model might be more or less appropriate for certain systems, but also make sure that they evaluate the model critically and understand its limitations. This Activity is an idea model meant to convey the concepts of exponential and logistic growth. It is not designed to be an accurate representation of any given system. It does, however, demonstrate one way that you can convey the ideas of exponential and logistic growth using simple rules for individuals, instead of using mathematical equations to describe the system level behavior. See Chapter 2 for a more in-depth discussion of idea models and minimal models for systems.

This Activity provides a good entry into creating simple StarLogo models. Try programming a model of exponential growth. How is the StarLogo model different from the penny model? A logistic growth model is a bit more complicated to create, but a basic logistic growth model can be built around the concepts of turtles-here and hatch. (Hint: You can limit the number of turtles on any given patch to one and hatch newborn turtles only if there are adjacent empty patches for the new offspring to inhabit.)

You may be surprised to learn that many researchers have used coins to augment *thought experiments*. A good place to read more about these kinds of experiments is Schelling (1978).

Turning Turtles Into Termites

There are many types of interactions that can occur between creatures and their environment. In this Challenge, you can choose to model one of two different types of interactions. You can create a project in which turtles alter their behavior based on environmental characteristics, or you can design and build a project in which turtles change their environment.

If you choose the first option, then create a project in which the environment influences the turtles in more than one way. Start by thinking about new ways that the environment can change turtle behavior. You might build a world of patches that affect the turtles' position, color, or speed in different ways. Your project should be more ambitious than the one you completed for Challenge 3. To see an example of this kind of project, check out *Speeding Bumper Turtles*.

If you choose the second option, then build a project that asks the turtles to manipulate the patches in their environment. Perhaps your turtles will "move" objects (represented by patches) as in the *Turtledozers* or *Termites* projects. Alternatively, your turtles could change the patch colors as they walk across the **Graphics Canvas**. You can explore how these modifications to the environment change the turtles' behavior.

EXPLORATIONS

POSSIBLE

◆ Try programming the turtles to draw paths in colors that also influence their movement.

◆ Experiment with combining turtle and patch activity. Perhaps patches of a certain color influence turtles and turtles change the color of each patch they walk across.

◆ What happens in your project if the patches change color randomly?

◆ See what happens if turtles multiply when they run into certain patches. Are the effects of **hatch** and **sprout** identical?

◆ Explore the results if patches affect absolute headings instead of relative headings.

◆ Think about some real-world systems in which living things interact with their environment. Try to incorporate some of those ideas in your project.

CHALLENGE PHILOSOPHY

In Challenge 3, you started to think about ways in which the environment can influence the behavior of individuals. Now you can begin to consider scenarios in which individuals also influence the environment. For instance, beavers build dams, changing the course of rivers; people cut down forests, altering the amount of available light and potential habitats; and termites eat wood, dramatically changing the stability of the original structure.

Often the changes that individuals make to their environment in turn influence the behavior of those same individuals. Imagine a teenager who doesn't pick up his dirty clothes. The more clothes that accumulate on the floor, the bigger the cleanup job that he faces, and the less likely he is to pick up all of his clothes. In this Challenge, you will learn to combine the effects of individuals on their environment with the effects of the environment on those individuals.

In the previous Challenge, a simple mechanism (check-patches) allowed the turtles to react to objects in the environment. If a turtle saw a blue patch in front of it, then it turned right. This Challenge introduces a mechanism for the turtles to manipulate their environment, allowing you to explore two-way interactions between the patches and the turtles.

There are two possible strands to follow in this Challenge. The first strand requires you to think creatively and devise new ways for the environment to affect turtle behavior. During this process, you will be able to explore the states (color, heading, etc.) of individual turtles. In the second strand, you will design and implement turtle behaviors that alter the environment. The ability to produce interactions between individuals and their environment opens the door to an incredibly rich area of modeling. The sample projects and commands provided in this Challenge only scratch the surface of possibilities. Feel free to explore these types of interactions at length, but remember that the parallel nature of StarLogo causes the complexity of your project to increase rapidly, so it is always better to start with a simple idea.

MODELING CONCEPTS

- Investigate ways that individuals can alter their environment.

- Understand how the environment can affect the behavior of individuals.

- Relate communication between individuals and their environment to real-world systems in which agents' interactions with the environment are important.

CHALLENGE DESCRIPTION

In this Challenge, you explore complex interactions between turtles and their environment. You can implement new ways that the patches can affect turtle behaviors or program the turtles to change their environment. As you explore these two options, you can also think about ways to combine turtle and patch activity. Before you begin programming, think about the kinds of environmental changes you would like to implement and how turtle actions might, in turn, be impacted by those changes.

STARLOGO CONCEPTS

- Learn simple commands that enable patches and turtles to communicate.

- Experiment with feedback between the turtles and patches.

- Teach turtles to change features of the patches that they occupy.

The sample projects in this Challenge contain combinations of interactions between turtles and their environment. As you think about different ways that turtle behavior can be influenced by the environment, you can explore the sample project *Speeding Bumper Turtles*. As you consider ways that turtles can change their environment, take a look at *Turtledozers*. The *Termites* project demonstrates how a StarLogo model can capture some elements of real-world systems.

CHALLENGE GUIDELINES

By now you should be comfortable building a simple StarLogo project from scratch. In this Challenge you are not provided with a preprogrammed starting project or piece of StarLogo code. Please be aware that it is perfectly OK—and sometimes preferable—to copy parts of past projects or simply look at their code if you find it helpful. In fact, that's why StarLogo was designed with visible procedures, even for the sample projects.

You have already encountered interface elements and many of the commands that you will use in this Challenge. A few new patch-related commands are covered below to help you create rich interactions between the turtles and patches. You might want to check out some of the sample projects before you get started on the Challenge. The first project demonstrates a new way to change the turtles' responses to their environment. The other two projects illustrate different ways that turtles can alter their environment.

Speeding Bumper Turtles

This project introduces the simple use of sliders to control how the turtles react to obstacles in their environment. In any model, sliders control values that anyone can easily change. Often, even a small change in a slider will cause a noticeable change in how the whole system looks or behaves.

The Speeding Bumper Turtles project.

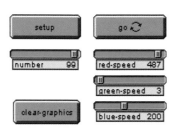

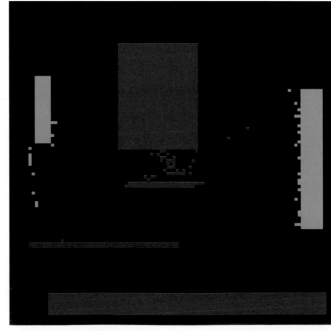

Speeding Bumper Turtles is similar to the **Bumper Turtles** project in the previous Challenge, except that in this project the turtles' speeds change every time they bounce off of a colored obstacle. The speed associated with each obstacle is determined by the corresponding slider value. Take a look at the procedures to see how this behavior is implemented. Remember, every time you see **red-speed**, **green-speed**, or **blue-speed** in the procedures code, the program is reading the current value from the corresponding slider.

Click the setup button to set up the turtles at their initial positions. Click the go button to start the simulation. At any time, you can change the value of each of the speed sliders, green-speed, red-speed, and blue-speed. The value of each slider determines the speed that the turtles assume after they bounce off of a colored patch. You can also set the number slider to determine the number of turtles in the project. This change takes effect only when you setup the simulation again. If you want to draw a new set of obstacles, press clear-graphics and draw new obstacles using the **Paint Tools**. According to the existing procedures, the obstacles need to be blue, red, or green for the turtles to react to them, but you can make the obstacles in any shape or location that you wish.

Turtledozers

This project is another variation of **Bumper Turtles**. Press setup to draw three randomly placed colored squares on the screen. If you want to, you can supplement these squares with additional drawings that you make using the **Paint Tools**. In **Turtledozers** the **check-patches** procedure has been modified so that when the turtles bounce off of an obstacle they drag a piece of it with them for one step. This turtle action disperses the obstacles. The three monitors keep track of the number of red, blue, and green patches. As the turtles disperse the obstacles, the number of colored patches eventually decreases. Why do you think that this happens?

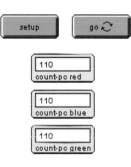

The Turtledozers' Interface.

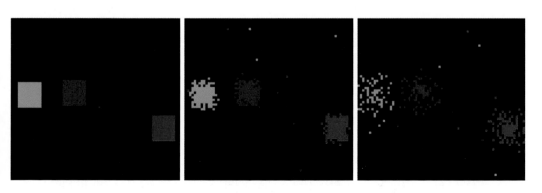

Turtledozers' Graphics Canvas over time.

Termites

This project is an idea model that was inspired by the behavior of termites gathering wood chips into piles (see Chapter 2 for more on idea models). Though the project does not capture all of the complexity of real termite behavior, it does allow you to visualize one simplified aspect of termite behavior—mound building.

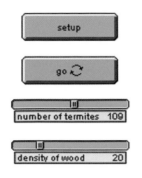

Click the setup button to set up the termites (red) and wood chips (yellow). The number slider controls the number of termites, and the density slider controls the initial density of wood chips. (Note: Changes in the number and density sliders only take effect when you press setup.) Click the go button to start the simulation. What happens to the distribution of the wood chips? What happens to the number of piles? Over time some piles disappear as termites carry away all of the chips. However, there is no way to start a new pile from scratch, since termites always put down their wood chips near other wood chips. Therefore the number of piles has to decrease over time.

What rules do you think the turtles are following? You might think that the termites would need a complicated set of rules to build piles. In fact, these termites follow a set of simple rules. Each termite starts wandering randomly. If it bumps into a wood chip, it picks the chip up and continues to wander randomly. When it bumps into another wood chip, it finds a nearby empty space and puts its wood chip down. (Notice that the wood chips are represented as colored patches. The appearance of movement comes from the termites updating the patch colors as they pick up and put down the wood chips.) As piles of wood chips begin to form, the piles are not "protected" in any way. That is, termites sometimes take chips away from existing piles. That strategy might seem counterproductive. Can you imagine what would happen if the piles were protected? How would you establish which piles should be protected?

The termites in this project employ a decentralized strategy to pile up the wood chips. There is no termite in charge and no special predesignated site for piles. In fact, the termites know nothing about creating large piles of wood chips. The termites only know how to set a single wood chip down next to another one. Each termite follows a set of simple rules, but the colony as a whole accomplishes a rather sophisticated task.

The Termites' Graphics Canvas over time.

 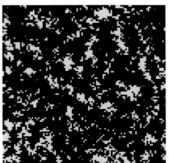 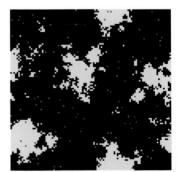

Asking Turtles and Patches

In StarLogo, all three characters, the turtles, the patches, and the observer, can communicate with one another. In addition, the observer can ask the other two characters to perform tasks. For example, it is often convenient to run a setup procedure from the **Observer Procedures Pane** that creates turtles and then asks them all to set their heading to 90, using **crt 100 ask-turtles [seth 90]**. In this case, the observer is asking all of the turtles to run the **seth 90** code. Similarly, the observer can ask all of the patches to change their color to red, using **ask-patches [setpc red]**. The observer is the only character that has this power; **ask-patches** and **ask-turtles** cannot be called by the turtles or the patches, and should be typed only in the **Observer Command Center** or **Procedures Pane** .

Here are some new commands that you may find useful as you create your own project.

If you want to...	Use these commands:	For this character:
Have a turtle set the color of a patch that it is on	Use the command **stamp** *newcolor* to change the color of the patch to *newcolor*, where *newcolor* is either one of the basic color names or a color number.	
Change the color of the patches	Use the command **setpc** *newcolor*. For example, you could type ask-patches [setpc blue] or ask-patches [setpc 101].	Note: This command must be called from within an **ask-patches** statement.
Have new turtles "born" on a patch	Patches can create turtles using the **sprout** [*statements*] command. The *statements* are any commands you wish to give the newborn turtles. You can specify that only certain patches create turtles. For example: ask-patches [if pc = 15 [sprout [setc blue]]] creates blue turtles on patches whose color equals 15.	Note: This command must be called from within an **ask-patches** statement.
Have turtles "give birth" to new turtles	Turtles can create new turtles using the **hatch** [*statements*] command. The newborn turtle is identical to the "mother" turtle. You can give specific commands to the new turtle in the *statements*.	

CHALLENGE HINTS

TIPS FOR TEACHERS

Challenge 4 suggests two different strands for students to pursue. The first, creating new ways in which the patches influence the turtles' behavior, is suitable for students who are still mastering some of the concepts from Challenge 3. Encourage these students to fully explore this aspect of the Challenge. This process will help to increase their proficiency with StarLogo without causing them to fall behind. If they are interested in manipulating the environment, but not quite ready to move to the second strand, they can make use of the **Paint Tools** to create an appealing environment for their project. Other students who may choose this first strand are those who had a great project idea during Challenge 3 but were unable to fully implement it in the time that they had. The second strand, instructing the turtles to change aspects of the environment, is good for those students who are comfortable with many ways that turtles can react to the environment and are excited about adding new kinds of behaviors to their models.

As students design, build, and present their projects for Challenge 4, ask them to think about the people who will use their projects. Are their ideas clearly communicated by their models? Do their projects attempt to address too many issues? Have they incorporated ways for people to interact with their models? If so, do these interactions illuminate the core ideas of their projects? Could a user understand and explain these core ideas? While not all students will be at this stage, your input can help them begin to consider these aspects of design. You can ask them to include instructions and explanations for using their projects in the **Information Window**.

Up until this point, students' flexibility in the StarLogo environment was limited. Now they know enough to build projects based on ideas that they have rather than just exploring a very basic set of commands. From now on, it is possible for you to customize the Challenges for your curriculum. When you hand out the Challenge, give students some ideas or sample solutions that are appropriate for your subject area. Ask them to address some domain-specific questions during their work-in-progress reports. See Chapter 5 for some ideas about customized projects. If you would like to find out more about how other teachers are adapting the Challenges for their classes, send email to the **starlogo-users@media.mit.edu** mailing list.

Survival of the Fittest Paper Catchers

In the previous Activity, you examined the population growth of pennies. This time the students themselves are the members of a growing population. This model incorporates a few new ideas about population growth models and also provides an opportunity for comparing two models of the same phenomenon.

MODELING CONCEPTS

◆ Explore a different model of population growth.

◆ Compare different approaches to modeling similar phenomena.

◆ Incorporate natural selection into the discussion of population growth.

MATERIALS

◆ A piece of scrap paper for every participant

◆ A newspaper

◆ Notepad or blackboard to record population dynamics

RUNNING THE ACTIVITY—PART 1

In the first stage of this Activity, ask everyone to crumple up a piece of (scrap) paper. Pick one person to come up to the front of the room and be the initial member of the population. Members of this population should follow these rules:

❶ If you are standing at the front of the room, then throw your paper high in the air (at least several feet above your head) when the facilitator gives the "next generation" command.

❷ If you catch your paper, then you survive and may "reproduce" by calling up another member of the audience to join the population.

❸ If you don't catch your paper, then you "die" and must sit down.

Lead participants through several "generations." If the population crashes or becomes extinct (because all of the population members drop their pieces of paper), begin again, noting that sometimes populations will crash by chance or become extinct when their numbers are small. Record the size of the population over time. What is the maximum population?

Once the members of the audience are all standing at the front of the room, take a look at the graph of the population over time. Ask the participants to reflect on some of the following issues:

• What type of population growth is modeled, and why does it occur?

• The growth curve changes shape dramatically when all potential members of the group are already in the population. What does this limitation add to (or take away from) the model?

• How realistic is the implementation of "death" in this model?

• How does chance play a role in this model? How does the inclusion of randomness make this model different from the penny growth model?

RUNNING THE ACTIVITY—PART 2

Now place a newspaper-sized piece of paper on the ground. Follow the same rules you did earlier, adding one new rule:

❹ Each member of the population must have part of one foot on the paper at all times. Removing your foot from the paper (even for an instant) results in "death" (sitting back down).

Proceed, as in the last experiment, by calling up one initial population member and asking that person to throw the paper in the air. Continue propagating new generations, noting the number of people in the population over time. What happens to this population? Is everyone able to stand on the paper?

When the population size stabilizes, discuss the implications of this new feature.

- Hold up the paper and show participants what they did to the "environment."

- What kind of growth does this model demonstrate?

- What kinds of death processes are modeled by implementing "dying" when you take your foot off the paper? How does this relate to limited resources in nature?

- Calculate a carrying capacity (maximum number of individuals supported) for this environment.

- Is there a newspaper size that leads to oscillating populations (many people die when the paper is crowded, which frees up a lot of space for growth, which fills up the paper, and so on)?

Compare the birth and death processes in this model and the penny growth model. What are the advantages and disadvantages of the two models? When would it be more appropriate to use one or the other?

FACTS FOR FACILITATORS

It is likely that people were cooperating in order to avoid collisions when they were standing close together on the newspaper. How do social factors like this one influence population dynamics?

Depending on the paper-catching skills of the people in the group, you might need to adjust how high the population members throw their papers. You might also use throwing height as a variable in the model. For a description of a similar activity and additional explorations, see Byington (1997).

Modeling a growing population is one avenue for exploration in Challenge 5. You and your students can consider the many different ways to model a single phenomenon and weigh the advantages and disadvantages of each approach.

State of the Turtles

In the previous Challenges, you altered several turtle properties (e.g., **heading**, **color**, etc.). These properties, called turtle variables or *states*, allow the turtles to remember information. Turtles can remember additional information about themselves if you add new turtle variables.

Can you create a StarLogo project with a turtle **energy** variable? How will your turtles gain and lose **energy**? How might your turtles' behaviors or looks change as their **energy** levels increase or decrease? How does the turtles' behavior help you visualize their changing states? What assumptions do you make about a turtle's states based on its behavior? Are your assumptions accurate?

For hints on getting started, check out the sample projects *Energizer Turtles* and *Rabbits*.

EXPLORATIONS

POSSIBLE

◆ Explore different ways that **energy** can affect the speed and heading of the turtles.

◆ Try having more than one factor (e.g., colored patches, x-coordinate, **who** number) influence the turtles' **energy**.

◆ See what happens if turtles with different **energy** levels affect the environment in different ways.

◆ Experiment with turtles hatching other turtles when their **energy** reaches a threshold level.

◆ Think about how the turtle behavior that you observe gives you clues about the underlying turtle states. What assumptions do you make about the turtle's states based on the observed behavior? How might you change your project to make the correlation between underlying states and overt behavior more instructive? For example, you could make turtles with more **energy** move faster.

◆ How can you use variables in your model to make individual behaviors seem more lifelike?

CHALLENGE PHILOSOPHY

Every January, the President of the United States delivers the State of the Union Address in which he describes the status of the country. Typically, he addresses a number of different topics, including the budget, crime, education, health care, and taxes. He provides information on how well the country is performing in each of these areas. For instance, in 1999 crime was falling to record lows while health care costs were increasing. The information he gives about each topic helps his constituents construct informed opinions about the status of the country. Just as the President describes the condition of the country, the status of other systems can also be described or assessed by looking at the underlying components. For example, your doctor weighs you, takes your temperature and blood pressure, and measures your cholesterol levels. Collecting information about each of these states helps her create a picture of your general health and well-being.

Often without even being conscious of it, you think about the states of organisms or whole systems. As you observe behaviors in the world, you might make guesses about the reasons underlying these behaviors. Think about the last time you were "people watching." If you saw a woman in a business suit running to catch a bus, you might have assumed that she was worried about being late for work. If you saw a young man pacing in front of a movie theater, you might have assumed that he was concerned because his date was late. If you saw a small child throwing a temper tantrum, you might have assumed that he was tired or hungry. In each of these cases, you were drawing conclusions about people's internal states based upon the behavior that you observed. Often, internal states—like being concerned, worried, tired, or hungry—influence the ways that people act. All creatures and objects, even subatomic particles, are affected by their internal states. Modeling the internal states of individuals provides you with an opportunity to understand a great variety of real-world systems.

When introducing new variables (or states) for the turtles in your StarLogo models, it is often helpful to envision an animal or object that you are trying to describe. Perhaps you are thinking about simulating a real turtle walking around. Such a turtle might have variables like speed, stamina, age, size, and so on. Once you have identified these variables you have arrived at the first difficult moment—deciding which of these are the most important for what you are modeling. When constructing models in StarLogo, as in many modeling programs, less is more. It is better to determine which variables are most useful and interesting in the context of your model than it is to try to incorporate too many variables. Adding too many variables can make it difficult to interpret or analyze your model. It is usually a good idea to start by picking one turtle variable with which to work. In this example, speed might be particularly relevant, so you could implement that variable.

MODELING CONCEPTS

- ◆ Explore ways that individuals react to their internal states.

- ◆ Investigate how altering creatures' internal states leads to modifications in their behavior.

- ◆ Experiment with methods for deducing individuals' internal states based on their observable behaviors.

- ◆ Relate the use of turtle variables and states to variables and states in real-world systems.

STARLOGO CONCEPTS

- ◆ Learn about existing turtle variables and how to use them.

- ◆ Create and modify your own turtle variables.

- ◆ Identify patch and global variables.

Keep in mind that turtle actions can be described at two different levels. On the top level, you can describe a turtle's actions in a model by watching what it does when the simulation is running. On the bottom level, you can look at the rules and states that determine the turtle's actions by reading the project code or looking inside the turtle to examine its states. You can think about turtle behaviors from the perspective of either of these two levels. Since turtle behaviors are based on rules and variables that you create, you can think about building those behaviors from the "bottom up." Or you can spend time observing the turtles' behavior from the "top down." As you watch the turtles, you might be able to make assumptions about their underlying rules or states based on your observations. This process of concurrently building behaviors from the bottom up and investigating behaviors from the top down is a great way to start thinking more deeply about the models that you are building in StarLogo.

CHALLENGE DESCRIPTION

By now you have played with most of the basic turtle variables including turtle number (**who**), **heading**, **color**, **xcor**, and **ycor**. Every turtle in each of your projects has all of these properties. With just these few properties you have managed to do some fantastic things with the turtles. Now you will learn how to add your own variables to the turtles, giving you and your turtles even more flexibility.

In this Challenge, you add the variable **energy**. Your task is to think of a creative project that uses this variable. The value of a turtle's **energy** could change when it runs into a special patch in the environment. Alternatively, you could implement spontaneous **energy** changes in your project. The changes in a turtle's **energy** should have some perceptible effect on its behavior. You might find that it helps to think of objects that have energy (e.g., bouncing electrons or foraging lizards) when deciding how to use this variable. Or you might choose to give your turtles **energy** first and then see what it can make them do. Both approaches are useful and can be effective.

CHALLENGE GUIDELINES

Turtle Monitors

The technique of adding turtle variables is not difficult, but using them effectively can be a bit of a challenge (no pun intended!). This concept may be easier to understand if you first think about turtle variables that already exist. Create some turtles and double-click on a turtle to bring up its **Turtle Monitor**.

A Turtle Monitor.

The **Turtle Monitor** lists and tracks the values of all of the turtle variables. You will notice that the turtle already has certain variables like **color**, **xcor** and **ycor** (the x- and y-coordinates respectively), **heading**, and so forth that enable the turtle to keep track of things like what it looks like and where it is going. Click on the value for **color**, type in a new value (or name) for **color** inside the **Turtle Monitor**, and then press Return to see the effect of your change 🍎. What happened to your turtle?

Each turtle knows the values of its own variables and can ask other turtles about the values of their variables (you will see this in a later Challenge). In addition to the predefined turtle variables, you can add your own variables if you want your turtles to keep track of additional information.

Creating Turtle Variables

You create turtle variables by typing **turtles-own** [*variablenames*] at the top of the **Turtle Procedures Pane**. *variablenames* are the one-word names used to identify the new turtle variables and should be separated by spaces. For example, if you would like to create turtle variables for **energy**, **age**, and **gender**, you would use the statement:

   turtles-own [energy age gender]

In this example, the variables **energy**, **age**, and **gender** are created for every turtle. Notice that there are spaces, not commas, between the variables and that you must list the variables in between square brackets. Make sure that you put all of your turtle variables on a single line. The following code will **not** work correctly:

   turtles-own [energy]
   turtles-own [age]
   turtles-own [gender]

turtles-own should be typed only once in any project.

Monitoring Turtle Variables

Try creating a turtle variable **energy** and setting it to a value (see the hints below). You can check the value of this variable for any turtle by opening its **Turtle Monitor**. Here is a **Turtle Monitor** showing values for **energy** as well as the turtles' standard variables (**color**, **heading**, and so forth.).

Some of the tasks you might want to accomplish with your new variables can be implemented using the following commands. The commands on the next page are based on the sample turtle variable **energy** and can only be executed by the turtles.

A Turtle Monitor with an energy variable.

If you want to...	Use these commands:	For this character
Create a new variable energy for all turtles	The statement **turtles-own [energy]** creates a new variable **energy** and allows you to use the set of commands that manipulate the turtles' **energy**.	This statement should be placed at the top of the **Turtle Procedures Pane**.
Set the value of energy for all turtles	The command **setenergy** *value* sets the variable **energy** to the *value* specified. Note that **setenergy** is one word.	
Increase the value of energy for all turtles	The command **setenergy energy +** *increase* adds the amount *increase* to the current energy level. Note that this is really the same as the last entry (**setenergy** *value*) with the *value* equal to the current **energy** plus an *increase*. Also, note the spaces on both sides of the plus sign.	
Do something to a turtle if its energy is above some value	Use the command **if energy >** *check* **[***statements***]** to cause turtles with an **energy** value greater than *check* to perform the *statements*.	

Multiply the energy of turtles who satisfy a certain condition	Use the statement
	  if *condition*
	    [setenergy energy * *multiplier***]**
	to ask those turtles who satisfy the *condition* to multiply their **energy** by the *multiplier*.
	Try: **if color = blue [setenergy energy * 1.5].**	

(left margin, vertical text) **CHALLENGE HINTS**

While these hints just show commands for the sample variable **energy**, you can use them for any variable that you create. For instance, if you created a variable called **age** you could use the command **setage**. For a complete list of the commands that are created for a new variable, check out the StarLogo Documentation section on variables at **http://www.media.mit.edu/starlogo/documentation/variables.htm**.

Patch and Global Variables

In addition to turtle variables, there are two other types of variables in StarLogo. Patch variables provide patches with the same ability to store information as turtle variables provide for turtles. If you are interested in implementing patch variables, you can read about them in the StarLogo Documentation.

The observer controls global variables that are not associated with patches or turtles. While every turtle or every patch keeps track of values for each turtle or patch variable, only one value exists for a global variable at any given time. An example of a global variable that you could create is time, as the value of time is usually the same for every object in the model. Integrating multiple variable types in a single project is a complicated endeavor. We recommend starting with turtle variables, which are the focus of this Challenge.

Energizer Turtles

A straightforward example of using a variable is shown in the project *Energizer Turtles*. This project builds on the *Bumper Turtles* series of projects. In this case when the turtles walk over patches of different colors their energy either increases or decreases, depending on the color of the patch that they pass. The turtles gain energy if they step on a red or yellow patch. They lose energy if they step on a blue or gray patch. The energy level of each turtle is indicated by its color (a more energetic turtle is brighter) as well as by how fast it moves (a more energetic turtle moves faster).

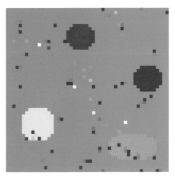

Energizer Turtles' Graphics Canvas.

As you explore this project, there are a couple of details to notice in the procedures. First, a modified check-patches procedure asks each turtle to increase or decrease its energy depending on the patch color at its location. Second, a turtle's energy affects both its color and its speed. The fd command uses the value of the turtle's energy variable to determine the size of the turtle's forward step each time it moves. The scale-color command sets the turtles with the most energy to almost white and the least energy to almost black, with the turtles in between showing varying shades of blue. The scale-color command takes four arguments (or inputs), so it is worth a quick look. This program uses the following command:

  scale-color blue energy 0 20

This command literally means, scale the color of the turtles to a shade of blue, depending on the value of the energy variable, with an energy value of 0 resulting in very dark blue and 20 in very light blue.

To try this project, click the setup button to create the number of turtles shown on the number slider. You can add "energy-change patches" by drawing red, yellow, blue, or gray patches. Click the go button to start the simulation and see the effect of the colored patches on the color and the speed of the turtles. You may notice that turtles tend to get stuck in some of the patches that decrease their energy. Can you modify the percentage increase or decrease in the turtles' energy (in the Turtle Procedures) to change this tendency?

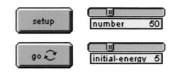

Energizer Turtles' Interface.

Rabbits

Another project that uses the energy concept is ***Rabbits***. This project explores a simple ecosystem made up of rabbits and grass. The rabbits wander around randomly, and the grass grows randomly. Rabbits use up **energy** as they move. When a rabbit bumps into some grass, it eats the grass and gains **energy**. If the rabbit gains enough **energy**, then it "reproduces" by hatching a new rabbit. If it loses all of its **energy**, then the rabbit dies.

Rabbits' Interface.

Click the setup button to set up the rabbits (red) and grass (green). The number slider controls the initial number of rabbits. Click the go button to start the simulation. The hatch-threshold slider sets the energy level at which the rabbits reproduce. The grass-rate slider controls the rate at which the grass grows. (Note: You cannot change the grass-rate in the middle of a simulation. The change takes effect at the next setup.)

Watch the total-rabbits monitor to see how the rabbit population changes over time. At first, there is not enough grass for the rabbits, and many rabbits die. But this allows the grass to grow more freely, providing an abundance of food for the remaining rabbits. These rabbits gain **energy** and reproduce. The abundance of rabbits leads to a shortage of grass, and the cycle begins again. Lotka (1925/1956) and Volterra (1926) originally characterized these patterns using a set of differential equations. If you would like to see a graph of these patterns, you can look at the **Plot Window** (in Challenge 8 you will learn to create your own graphs). In order to fit the number of rabbits and the amount of grass on the same scale, the plot shows the number of rabbits and one-fifth of the amount of grass. What happens to the number of rabbits and amount of grass over time? What does this imply for the long-term stability of this population of rabbits and grass? Try manipulating the parameters to change these oscillations.

In this model, a single rabbit is able to reproduce, hatching new rabbits whenever its energy level exceeds the threshold. Obviously, this process is an oversimplification of the way that real rabbits reproduce. Some people find it difficult to accept this simplified model of rabbit reproduction. The sample project, ***Rabbits***, is an idea model (see Chapter 2) of rabbits and grass interacting in an ecosystem. It does not attempt to recreate all of the complexity of a real ecosystem. Instead it focuses on just a few relationships (between the rabbits and their food). One way to conceptu-

Rabbits' Graphics Canvas over time.

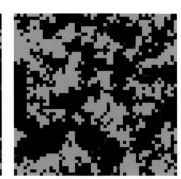

alize these simplified rabbits is to think of them as "wrabbits," where the silent "w" differentiates between a real rabbit and an abstract, simplified version of a rabbit (a wrabbit) that embodies just a few characteristics of a real rabbit.

No matter how hard you try, you will not be able to model everything about a real rabbit (or any organism) in your projects. Instead, it is best to focus on the essential parts of your model, by thinking about what you want to investigate or explore. In this case, the model focuses on the way that **energy** is incorporated into the system. This implementation of wrabbits succeeds in showing the relationship between food depletion and population growth, even though the model of reproduction is not realistic. The person who built this model *could* have included other rabbit characteristics, but sometimes, additional complexity can make a model less comprehensible. Remember that idea models can be very effective for exploring the dynamics of a particular concept. Chapter 2 includes a detailed discussion of this and other pertinent modeling issues.

TIPS FOR TEACHERS

In Activity 5, Survival of the Fittest Paper Catchers, students explore a model of population growth. That model incorporates simple strategies for implementing reproduction and fitness in a model (catching the piece of paper while keeping a foot on the newspaper). Students might consider ways to model similar processes, like fitness or reproduction, in a StarLogo project. Perhaps when their turtles reach a certain energy level, they are able to hatch new turtles. Of course, students will want to think about the states of the newly hatched turtles (i.e., How much **energy** do they have? What is their age?). They might also explore what kind of population growth occurs in that model. Regulating the total amount of available **energy** in the environment (like regulating the size of the paper or the ability of the paper catchers) can have a dramatic impact on the rate of population growth.

During their work-in-progress reports, students should be able to articulate how and why the turtles' energy levels change and describe the effects that those changes have on the turtles' behavior. They should also be able to describe how one could hypothesize about the level of **energy** that a turtle possesses by observing the turtle's actions. Students should be able to give a rational explanation for the turtle behavior that they created. Some of these explanations might draw parallels to the states of creatures in the real world (like hunger, age, or happiness).

ACTIVITY 6

Sold! to the Highest Bidder

Imagine that you just opened a bread store. You need to set bread prices high enough to pay all of your employees, meet your expenses, and (hopefully) make a profit. On the other hand, if you set prices too high, then you are likely to drive away customers. To run a successful store you must make certain predictions about your customers' behavior. You need to predict how many customers you can serve, how many loaves of bread they will buy per week, how much they will pay for your bread, and how loyal they will be if you later raise prices. As you determine the price of each item, you must consider all of these competing factors. How much can you charge for a loaf of bread before your customers will buy their bread elsewhere?

Of course, you don't own the only bread store in town. At the same time that you set prices for your bread, store owners down the block are making their own predictions about customers' behavior. They may price their bread lower or run specials to avoid losing customers during the opening week of your store. You will need to predict the duration of your competitors' promotions. Perhaps you will decide to match their deals, taking an initial loss but hoping to gain market share.

Though it seems quite straightforward, your ability to set an appropriate price for bread is governed by many competing factors, including the decisions of other people. Many systems display similar properties. Whether you are deciding how much to pay for a used car or if you will purchase a particular stock at its current price, you often weigh competing factors as you decide the value of a product. Of course, the final prices of these products are determined by the decisions of many people.

Auctions are one place where it is easy to see the process of many people making these kinds of decisions simultaneously. Though the factors they consider might not all be identical, participants at an auction are constantly deciding what the auctioned item is worth to them. No one person is operating alone. The interactions of all of the people determine the final value of an item—just like the interactions among you, your customers, and your competitors determine the ultimate price of the bread in your store. In this Activity people can participate in and reflect on a simple, yet surprising, price-setting game.

MODELING CONCEPTS

◆ Explore how simple rules can lead to unexpected results.

◆ Observe how interactions among rules affect overall system behavior.

◆ Investigate the dynamics of an auction.

MATERIALS

◆ A single dollar bill

RUNNING THE ACTIVITY

Show participants a crisp new dollar bill. Explain that you will sell this dollar bill to the highest bidder and that you will set the initial price at one penny. In addition to following standard auction practices, bidders must abide by these two rules:

❶ The highest bidder pays the winning bid and receives the dollar.

❷ The second-highest bidder pays his or her own highest bid yet receives nothing.

After making sure that participants understand how the rules of this auction differ from a standard auction, begin the bidding. Continue the auction until there are no more bids or until you reach a preset time limit.

What happened? You might pose the following questions:

- Was the selling price about what the participants expected? Why or why not?

- Did everyone bid? Who were the predominant bidders?

- Did bidders raise their bids by the same amount every time? If not, was there a pattern in the way that bids were raised?

- What factors did participants consider as they placed their bids? Did these factors change over the course of the auction?

- How would the dynamics of the auction change if participants were bidding on a hundred-dollar bill?

- Would the outcome be the same in a silent auction?

- What would happen if participants did not know the exact value of the item that they were bidding on? For instance, what if they were bidding on a black box that contained some amount between one and five dollars?

RUNNING THE ACTIVITY—EXTENSIONS

Ask participants to consider how their experiences in the dollar bidding game could change their understanding of other markets. Challenge them to predict the selling price of an item on an online auction site such as eBay. Have them track the bidding from start to finish.

- What dynamics arise in this system?

- Does the sale of similar items necessarily result in similar auction dynamics?

- Who were the major players in the auction? Did they exhibit any notable characteristics, such as previous bidding experience?

- How did the preset closing time influence the dynamics?

- Sometimes sellers set a price that must be met before a sale can occur. Usually bidders are unaware of this price. How does this constraint affect the dynamics?

Encourage participants to investigate other markets. Does the real estate market exhibit similar patterns? How does haggling at flea markets or used-car dealerships compare to other kinds of bidding? Can participants predict the future price of a stock? What features of the stock market set it apart from the other markets that they have explored?

FACTS FOR FACILITATORS

Make sure that participants believe that the two highest bidders will both have to ante up for the dollar. If they don't think that the game has real consequences, then they are likely to change the way that they bid. Also, make sure that participants don't share the results of this Activity with other groups. When participants possess knowledge about the outcome of the auction, the dynamics can dramatically change.

Though people sometimes believe that few general lessons can be learned from studying such a basic market, this Activity illustrates one way that the rules of a system can produce unexpected outcomes. For an in-depth look at modeling dynamic systems in a business context, see Sterman (2000).

In addition, social interactions and the predictions that individuals make about other people's behavior also affect the dynamics of this system. How did participants try to influence each other during the bidding process? What did participants think other people would do? Were their predictions correct? For more information on the social dynamics of decision making, see Levin (1999).

Teaching Turtles to Talk

They say that misery loves company and that there is safety in numbers. The turtles in this Challenge have their own clichés—"turtles love company" and "there is happiness in numbers." The turtles adopted these expressions because their **happiness** increases when they share a patch with another turtle.

To begin this Challenge you can explore the projects *Shiny Happy Turtles 1* and *Shiny Happy Turtles 2*, which demonstrate two different ways that a turtle can gain **happiness** when it shares a patch with another turtle. See if you can figure out how the turtles increase their **happiness** in these projects. What methods are used in each project to affect the turtle behavior? What patterns of behavior can you identify in each project?

Next, look at the heart of these two projects (the procedures **friends-meet** and **set-avghappy**) and create your own project that enables turtles to affect the **happiness** of other turtles. You can try experimenting with *methods for* increasing and decreasing **happiness** or exploring the *effects of* increased or decreased **happiness**. Your Challenge is to create a project, incorporating principles from the sample projects, that enables turtles to influence each other's **happiness** and react to their own levels of **happiness**.

EXPLORATIONS

POSSIBLE

◆ Think of a situation in which turtles might be unhappy if there were other turtles nearby. Try to implement this in your project.

◆ Look at what happens if happiness causes turtles to slow down or move in a different pattern. What happens if happy turtles alter their environment?

◆ Can you think of any animals that are happy when they stick close together? Are there any costs or benefits from that behavior? How would you model that kind of system?

◆ Some organisms behave differently when they are crowded. Can you think of an example of this kind of behavior? Can you create a model to illustrate your example?

CHALLENGE PHILOSOPHY

It was cold and rainy outside when Talia got the call that her softball game was postponed. She decided to call some of her friends to see if they wanted to go see a movie instead. Unfortunately, no one was home. She left messages on her friends' answering machines asking them to meet her at the theater at 1:30 p.m. Talia headed out, hoping that some of her friends would get the message and meet her before the movie started. She arrived a little early, and none of her friends were there. As she waited in the lobby, she was a little worried that she would have to go the movie alone. A few minutes later she saw her friend Randy. She immediately perked up when she realized she was going to have some company. Within a few minutes three more of her friends arrived, each causing her mood to improve. By the time the movie began, six of Talia's friends were there, and she was very happy.

The interactions between Talia and her friends clearly affected Talia's mood—and probably her friends' moods too. Such effects, of course, are very common: The dynamics of many systems rely heavily on the interactions among individual members of the system. Creating models that include interactions among individuals, as well as interactions between individuals and their environment, can create wholly new dynamics. Sometimes, these dynamics cannot be predicted by looking at each of the interactions individually.

Interactions among turtles are one of the most powerful aspects of StarLogo, and they can get quite complicated. You will start by exploring some of the most straightforward turtle-turtle interactions. These interactions occur when two turtles land on the same patch and immediately exchange a single piece of information. In the upcoming Challenges, more advanced turtle-turtle interactions are described. Given the complexity of these concepts, and the amount of material covered so far, it is important to proceed slowly at this point. As you move forward, there will be ample opportunity to continue with and expand upon the ideas that are introduced in this Challenge.

MODELING CONCEPTS

◆ Explore ways of implementing interactions among individuals.

◆ Investigate how repeated interactions among turtles—like those caused by crowding or group living—influence the behavior that individuals exhibit towards one another.

◆ Discover how interactions among individuals can change the dynamics of the system.

STARLOGO CONCEPTS

◆ Learn how turtles can react to the presence of other turtles.

◆ Implement one way to facilitate turtle-turtle communication.

◆ Explore how turtles can get a single piece of information from another turtle (i.e., change turtles into a turtle).

CHALLENGE DESCRIPTION

This Challenge builds on concepts introduced in the previous Challenge. Challenge 5 introduced turtle states that were affected by the environment. You might have noticed that in *Energizer Turtles* some turtles became isolated and were unable to get out of areas that depleted their **energy**. In this Challenge, you will learn how to use turtle-turtle communication to rescue isolated turtles.

Two sample projects, each of which incorporates the idea of turtle **happiness**, are included in this Challenge. Each of the sample projects starts with the basic model that turtles increase or decrease their **happiness** based upon where they are—in school or at the movies. In addition, each project employs a mechanism that enables turtles to gain **happiness** when they meet other turtles. Spend some time exploring these models, both by playing with them and by looking at their underlying procedures. Relating the turtle-turtle interactions you observe in the simulation to the procedures that cause those interactions can be very informative (and sometimes difficult... have patience).

In these projects, a turtle's **happiness** is partially dependent on whether or not it is sharing a patch with another turtle. A turtle can also access the **happiness** of another turtle on its patch, compare the other turtle's **happiness** with its own, and change its own **happiness** accordingly. Once you have a feel for how to implement these simple turtle-turtle communications, you can integrate these interactions into your own projects.

CHALLENGE GUIDELINES

In this Challenge, you will play with some models that are related to the *Energizer Turtles* project from Challenge 5 but also include simple turtle-turtle interactions. These models are intended to help you visualize how turtle-turtle interactions work and provide some structure for implementing the commands used in these interactions. After some explorations, you will use the building blocks provided in this Challenge to create your own project with turtle-turtle interactions.

There are four turtle capabilities used in this Challenge:

1 A turtle knows how many other turtles are on its patch.

2 A turtle can react to turtles on its patch.

3 A turtle can find the **who** number of another turtle on its patch.

4 A turtle can ask for the value of another turtle's variables if it knows the other turtle's **who** number.

Together, these capabilities facilitate simple turtle-turtle interactions. The first two capabilities enable the simplest kind of turtle-turtle interaction and are demonstrated in the sample project *Shiny Happy Turtles 1*. In that project, each turtle checks to see if there is more than one turtle on its patch. If a turtle sees another turtle sharing its patch, the turtle doubles its happiness.

This communications algorithm is extended to include all four of these turtle capabilities in *Shiny Happy Turtles 2*. By enabling a turtle to access the variables of another turtle on the same patch, this project allows two turtles to average their happiness when they meet.

Shiny Happy Turtles 1

This project builds on the principles introduced in the *Energizer Turtles* project from Challenge 5. The turtles in this project are born with a state of happiness (a turtle variable similar to energy in Challenge 5). Turtles' happiness can increase or decrease as they interact with their environment and with other turtles.

Two turtle-environment interactions are modeled in this project. When turtles are in the red "cinema" patches, they gain or lose happiness based on the settings in the cinema slider. Similarly, turtles gain or lose happiness in the blue "school" patches based on the value of the school slider.

Turtle-turtle interaction is also modeled in this project. When the turtles find themselves alone on a patch, they lose a small amount of happiness. But when turtles find themselves sharing a patch with another turtle, they double their happiness. The assumption underlying this model is that turtles are happier when they are in contact with other turtles.

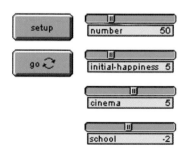

The Shiny Happy Turtles 1 project.

Turtles express their happiness in three ways. First, happier turtles move faster. Second, happier turtles are lighter in color (very light green as compared to dark green). Finally, happier turtles tend to circle to their right, aiming to get back to the place that made them happy, while unhappy turtles tend to keep moving in a straight line as they look for a more pleasant environment.

To start the simulation, click setup to create the number of turtles indicated on the number slider. Each turtle is created with a random level of happiness. You can adjust the maximum value using the initial-happiness slider. Click go to watch the turtles interact with each other and with their environment. You can change the influence exerted by the movies and the school by increasing or decreasing values of the school and cinema sliders. The slider values control the percentage of increase or decrease in happiness of a turtle when it occupies the school or cinema patches.

Take a look at what happens to turtles who become isolated in patches that are causing them to lose happiness. Sometimes they move away, but often they look stuck. In which patches do they tend to get stuck? Why? Investigate how changing the influence of the school and cinema patches affects this pattern. Now examine the code. In particular, look at the procedure that causes the turtles to double their happiness when they meet other turtles. Try changing the number of degrees that happy turtles turn or modifying the amount of happiness that lonely turtles lose. How does each of these changes affect the patterns you observe in the simulation?

Shiny Happy Turtles 2

The interface and most of the principles of *Shiny Happy Turtles 2* are exactly the same as those in *Shiny Happy Turtles 1*. Play with *Shiny Happy Turtles 2* for a little while. Can you tell what is different about this project based on your observations of the turtle-turtle and turtle-environment interactions? What unique patterns can you identify in this project?

In *Shiny Happy Turtles 2*, when two turtles share a patch they average their two happiness values (and add 10 percent for good fortune). These turtle-turtle interactions can lead to noticeably different patterns than the kind you observed in *Shiny Happy Turtles 1*. Watch what happens when a really happy turtle meets a really unhappy turtle. A good place to look for this is in a patch that causes turtles to lose happiness. What other kinds of interactions can you see in *Shiny Happy Turtles 2*?

You might want to examine the procedures in this second project. Only minor modifications were made to *Shiny Happy Turtles 1*. The procedure that doubled happiness has been changed to calculate the average happiness of the two turtles. Another procedure was added to set the happiness of the two turtles to their average happiness plus 10 percent. This procedure uses the one-of-turtles-here command to obtain the who number of another turtle and then uses the who number to access the happiness of that turtle.

Turtle-Turtle Commands

You will need the following commands to implement basic turtle-turtle interactions in your own projects.

If you want to...	Use these commands:	For this character:

Do one thing if a certain condition is satisfied, and do something else if that condition is not satisfied

The conditional
  ifelse *condition*
  [*statement1*] [*statement2*]
executes *statement1* if the stated condition is true and *statement2* if it is false. For example, the statement
  ifelse color = blue
  [rt 90] [lt 90]
causes all blue turtles to turn right 90 degrees and all other turtles to turn left 90 degrees.

depending on whether Turtle or Observer Commands make up *statement1* and *statement2*

Find out if there are any other turtles on a patch

The command count-turtles-here returns the number of turtles on a patch.

Get the who number of another turtle that is on your patch

The command one-of-turtles-here returns the who number of another turtle on a patch, if there is another turtle present. If there are no other turtles present, then –1 is returned.

Get the value of a variable from another turtle

Use the command
  set*variable1* (*variable2*-of one-of-turtles-here) to get a variable value from another turtle. *variable1* is the name of the variable you are using to store the value of *variable2* from the other turtle. For example:
  setotherage (age-of one-of-turtles-here)
stores the second turtle's age in the first turtle's variable otherage.

This code segment requires the following declaration of two turtle variables at the top of the **Turtle Procedures Pane**:
turtles-own [age otherage]

One note about turtles on patches: An individual turtle is always sitting on a patch, so there will always be *one* turtle on a patch (itself!) when you ask a turtle to look and see how many turtles occupy its patch (by using count-turtles-here). Therefore, if you are interested in identifying turtles who are sharing a patch with at least one other turtle, you will need to make sure that count-turtles-here is greater than one.

TIPS FOR TEACHERS

The commands in this Challenge are fairly complicated compared to those covered in earlier Challenges. For instance, some students might not be familiar with the concept of **ifelse** statements. The following real-world example might help them understand how this command works:

> If students score more than 80 percent on the next quiz, then they receive a prize; otherwise they must complete extra homework assignments.

See if they can write that instruction in StarLogo code, like this:

```
ifelse score > 80 [win_prize] [do_extra_homework]
```

If students are feeling overwhelmed, then suggest that they consult their classmates for help. Encourage your students to experiment with different implementations of the commands until they fully understand the range of functionality that these commands enable.

As your students begin to think about programming turtle-turtle interactions they are likely to develop very complex ideas for their projects. Initially, these ideas will be far more complex than they know how to implement right now. Make sure that they work on the simple interactions in this Challenge. If they master those interactions quickly, then encourage them to think of more ways that they can apply these interactions. During the work-in-progress reports, students can show their Challenge 6 solutions and discuss one or two possible extensions of their models. The upcoming Challenges introduce more advanced turtle-turtle interactions, and provide plenty of opportunity for students to build more complex models.

ACTIVITY 7

Foraging Frenzy

Imagine you are in the market for a car. Many factors will influence the kind of car you decide to buy: How much money you have now; how much money you plan to make in the near future; your ideal car's aesthetics; how much you will drive the car; the conditions in which you will drive the car; how long you plan to own the car; how much you want to drive a trendy car; and so on. As you evaluate each of these factors you will need to weigh their relative importance in order to come to a final decision.

Making complex decisions is a task people do many times a day—often without even realizing it. Which route will you take home? In which spot will you park? Which grocery store line will be the fastest? How will you allocate your time after dinner? As you weigh the costs and benefits for each decision, you get closer and closer to reaching the optimal solution for you. Complex decision making is not restricted to people. Many animals constantly make complex decisions of their own.

This Activity simulates the decision-making process of an animal foraging for food. Foraging animals consider many factors as they search for their next meal. How much time will they spend searching for food? What is the best place to find food? What kind of food will they look for? Unlike some of the decisions mentioned above, the decisions an animal makes about the food it gathers have a significant impact on its ability to survive and reproduce.

In this Activity, participants in a group take on the role of foraging animals. Their resource of choice is beans. Their goal is to gather as many beans from the feeding stations as they can in a given amount of time.

MODELING CONCEPTS

◆ Discover the challenges involved in assessing resource availability.

◆ Learn about some of the foraging decisions that animals must make when gathering resources.

◆ Study a simple model of optimization.

◆ Gain experience in formally analyzing the decision-making process.

MATERIALS

◆ (Uncooked!) kidney beans—about 1 pound per 10 participants

◆ Three stopwatches or digital watches

◆ Large notepad or blackboard for recording line lengths

◆ Jelly beans

CHALLENGE 7

Quest for Communication

In the project **Castle Invasion**, turtles try to gain entrance to a castle, but the entrance is protected with a code. In order to gain access, a turtle needs to know four code words. A turtle can learn these words by running over four colored patches that hold the secret words. Watch the turtles learn the code words. How long does it take them to get into the castle? What happens if more patches hold the secret words?

The turtles need to figure out a faster way to get back into the castle. Your Challenge is to help them work together so that they can enter the castle more quickly. By sharing the code words that they already know, the turtles can help each other get into the castle.

Using the command **grab**, you can instruct the turtles to exchange code words with one another. Try to determine if the enhanced information exchange affects how quickly the turtles can break into the castle. What happens if you modify the way that they exchange information? How does this change affect the time it takes them to gain access to the castle? The **Collisions** project illustrates a different use of **grab**.

EXPLORATIONS

POSSIBLE

◆ What happens if the turtles do not go directly to the castle once they know all four words? What else might you do with these turtles? How does this model compare to team projects in which no one person gets credit until the entire team has completed the project?

◆ Try making a model where turtles exchange information based on a certain probability.

◆ How do you think information exchange and eventual castle entry will be affected if the turtles occasionally forget words? Can you implement that modification?

◆ What if there were a cost (losing all of the known code words, dying, etc.) when a turtle tried to enter the castle without knowing all of the words?

◆ What happens to the length of time to castle entry if you change the number of turtles? What if you change the number of code words?

◆ Apply this type of turtle-turtle communication to other projects that you have been working on.

The turtle-turtle communication algorithms used to model this information transfer are powerful components of any modeling environment. Modeling interactions among creatures can enrich your existing models and broaden the scope of models you can create.

CHALLENGE PHILOSOPHY

Communication between individuals can take many forms. Unicellular organisms leave chemical trails that other cells can follow. Whales call to one another over great distances for reasons that scientists are still trying to understand. Colliding billiard balls transfer information about velocity and heading. All of these instances of information exchange have profound implications for the dynamics of the systems. Virtually every system that you encounter includes individual entities that communicate with one another. Think of a system and imagine what would happen if there were no communication among the elements of the system.

In modeling any kind of information exchange, you will need to consider how the information passes from one individual to another. Sometimes individuals need to communicate for an extended period of time. In other circumstances, communication occurs in short bursts. In this Challenge, you will learn advanced techniques to facilitate various forms of information exchange. These techniques will enable you to create models with rich interactions.

Conceptualizing information exchange is easy when you think about a single whale calling to another whale. But things get much more complicated in a parallel system, where many individuals interact all at once. In these systems, it is sometimes difficult to predict the consequences of many simultaneous exchanges of information. Since StarLogo is a parallel environment, you may find that your models exhibit increasing (and fascinating) complexity.

Timing is another aspect of parallel programming that you will need to consider. When you type **fd 1**, every single turtle on the screen moves forward one step at the same time. But if you have many instructions for the turtles to follow, it is possible that the turtles will get out of sync. This is not an error. It is the result of each turtle taking care of its own tasks in its own time (as opposed to having a centralized system in which an "overseer" makes all of the turtles do the same thing at exactly the same time). An actual population of turtles probably behaves in a similar manner, with each turtle acting independently much of the time.

MODELING CONCEPTS

◆ Build models with sustained communication between individuals.

◆ Investigate how different types of information exchange alter the dynamics of a system.

◆ Explore ways of integrating interactions among individuals with interactions between individuals and their environment.

STARLOGO CONCEPTS

◆ Practice implementing advanced turtle-turtle interactions.

◆ Use **grab** to communicate with another turtle.

◆ Access and modify other turtles' variables using **partner**.

depart having exchanged information about the first and second words. Adding the following commands will allow a turtle to get the first code word from another turtle who already knows it 🍎.

	In English this reads:

grab one-of-turtles-here
  [if (code1 = none) and
 	
  ((code1-of other) not= none)
 	
  [setcode1 code1-of partner
   setnumber number + 1]
  ]
	If there is another turtle here, grab that turtle and set your variable partner to that turtle's who number.
	If you don't know code1 and
	  if the other turtle does know code1,
	
	then learn code1 from your partner and increase the number of words you know by 1.

The grabbing turtle keeps the same **partner** until the end of the instruction list (the last square bracket ends the **grab** by releasing the turtle's **partner**).

You can add similar commands to enable the turtles to exchange the other three code words. Then, when turtles bump into one another, they will share all of the information that they have gathered.

The **grab** command is key to implementing turtle-turtle communication in your projects. Spend some time becoming comfortable with the Turtle Commands on the next page that are used to exchange information.

If you want to...	Use these commands:	For this character:
Talk to another turtle	The command **grab** *selectedturtle* [*statements*] allows a turtle to select a **partner** and then run the *statements*. *selectedturtle* is any command that returns a turtle's **who** number. A turtle only keeps his **partner** for the duration of the *statements*.	
Look at the variable of another turtle	The command *variable1-of whonumber* allows a turtle to inspect another turtle's *variable1*. *whonumber* can be a number or a command that returns a **who** such as **partner** or **one-of-turtles-here**. For example: **if ((color-of partner) = blue) [setc red]** allows a turtle to check to see if his **partner** is blue and, if so, change his own **color** to red. The parentheses are required in this command.	
Change another turtle's variable	The command *setvariable2-of whonumber newvalue* changes the other turtle's *variable2* to the *newvalue* you specify. For example, **setc-of 3 blue** changes the **color** of turtle three to blue.	
Execute commands if something is not true	Use a traditional **if** statement with the command **not=** to carry out instructions if a condition is not met. **if (color not= red) [*statement*]** runs the *statement* only if the turtle **color** is not red .	
Define a variable that takes word values instead of numeric values	The statement **turtles-own** [*variablename* [*word1 word2*]] creates a new variable *variablename*, and allows you to set its value to *word1* or *word2*. For instance, you can create a variable **transport** that can take on four possible values: **turtles-own [transport [car boat truck train]]**	

Collisions

This project is an idea model of a particle system that illustrates the use of **grab**. In **Collisions**, particles bounce off of walls and off of each other. They conserve energy, but not momentum, when they collide. Once a turtle has grabbed a **partner** in the **collide** procedure, it runs all of the instructions in between the square brackets. If a turtle doesn't find a **partner** to **grab**, then it skips all of those instructions and continues going.

Set the number slider to the desired number of particles, then press setup and go. Can you see any collisions? Is it any easier to track the collisions when the turtles' pens are down? When the turtles take large steps they sometimes jump over one another. Can you reduce their forward step size to eliminate this effect?

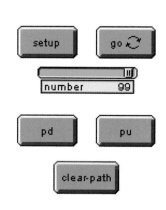

The Collisions' interface.

TIPS FOR TEACHERS

By now your students will have realized that incorporating communication into a system can cause significant changes in its dynamics. As your students learn a variety of ways to implement communication between creatures, it is important that they appreciate the different effects of each communication method. For instance, when the observer asks all of the turtles to change their colors to blue, the turtles all respond immediately irrespective of where they are on the **Graphics Canvas**. But, when individual turtles ask their partners to change their colors to blue, the effect is less immediate and less centralized.

Invite your students to recall 27 Blind Mice (Activity 2). In that Activity, they were initially able to engage in global communication by yelling out their numbers, resulting in the rapid and complete formation of groups. When they were restricted to whispering, the groups formed more slowly and were sometimes fragmented. Both of these forms of communication occur in real systems, and your students now have the ability to include them in their StarLogo models. Encourage your students to consider the methods of communication that they want to implement in their models and the effects that each implementation will have on the resulting dynamics.

It can be difficult for students to determine whether or not their turtles are successfully communicating with one another. Suggest that they incorporate temporary debugging code to test their communications procedures. For instance, they can insert a color change command into the **grab** statement so that they get visual feedback when one turtle grabs another. The code:

```
grab one-of-turtles-here [setc yellow setc-of partner red]
```

colors grabbing turtles yellow and their partners red. If no turtles are turning these colors, then communication is not taking place. Two ways to increase the frequency of turtle-turtle communication are to increase the density of turtles in a project or to set the turtles' forward step size to a number less than or equal to one (turtles who **jump** over one another never share the same patch, even if their paths cross).

grab is a powerful command that can be applied in many systems. Once students have mastered the process of grabbing a turtle and manipulating that turtle using the **partner** command, encourage them to integrate this process into other projects. If you are doing a final project in your class, workshop, or seminar, now is a good time to suggest that students begin thinking not only about the topic for their final project but also about how they want to build it. At this stage, we often encourage groups to create posters describing a few possible topics for their final projects. We suggest that they include two or three questions that they want to explore through their models. We display these posters around the room to encourage feedback and cross-pollination of ideas. Often we hold an extra work-in-progress session for students to present their posters to the whole group. This process can help groups solidify and refine their final project ideas.

Majority Rules

Newspapers, television reports, and Internet sites are filled with polls that report things like the most popular presidential candidate, the most popular soft drink, and the most popular car. As you read the results, you might wonder what these polls are based on. Often you were not consulted on your opinion about the candidates, soft drinks, or cars. In fact, you might be hard-pressed to find anyone who contributed his or her opinion to any of these polls. That is because these polls are based on small samples of people whose opinions pollsters believe represent those of the entire population.

Though the process may seem unreliable, people often make decisions based on information drawn from a small sample of people. If you are buying a new shirt and want to know whether or not it looks good on you, then you might ask the salespeople or your friends for their opinions. But you are unlikely to solicit the advice of everyone in the store. You can reach a decision about the shirt based on the opinions of a few people.

This Activity asks participants to examine the process of opinion formation based on their assessment of the available data. Participants try to adopt opinions that are held by the majority of the group. They refine their opinions by learning about the opinions of other people. The dynamics of opinion adoption are influenced by the number of people that each participant samples and the algorithms that participants use to evaluate their data.

MODELING CONCEPTS

◆ Explore the ways in which information informs decision making.

◆ Study the effects of sample size on the reliability of information.

◆ Demonstrate the dynamics that result from the local exchange of information.

MATERIALS

◆ Large notepad or blackboard for making graphs

◆ Post-It notes or small pieces of paper

RUNNING THE ACTIVITY

Ask participants to decide which color they prefer, blue or green, and then write down their choice on a Post-It note. Have them close their eyes and hold up their note to indicate which color they have chosen. Count the number of greens and blues and record the results out of the group's sight.

Next have the group open their eyes and start walking around randomly. As they meet people they should exchange their opinions by whispering their current choices to one another. After 15–20 seconds, ask them to stop, and challenge them to silently decide which opinion they believe is held by the majority, and then write that color on their Post-It note. Again, have them close their eyes and hold up their notes, so that you can count the number of greens and blues and record those numbers.

Repeat the process of group polling and recording the number of greens and blues. Make sure that no one peeks during the recording process, and make sure that participants always whisper the color that is currently on their Post-It note. Repeat this cycle about 10 times or until the group reaches consensus. Then allow the group to view a graph of the total counts of greens and blues that were recorded at each interval.

Discuss why the opinions evolved as they did. You might pose the following questions:

- Did the group ever reach consensus? If so, did it take as long as they thought it would? If not, why?

- Which color was initially more popular? Did that color remain the most popular or did the other color become more popular? Can the group propose any hypotheses to explain these dynamics?

- How did participants decide which color they chose before each group count? Did they always go with the majority from the group that they polled? Was there a tendency to stick with the color that they had already chosen? What rules did people use as they chose their colors? Can participants describe their decision-making process as a list of rules?

- Did the graph of opinion adoption reflect their intuitions about the system? What data might have aided their understanding of the system? For instance, what if they had knowledge about how many people each participant was sampling?

Try running this Activity again, but allow participants to keep their eyes open during the group count. This modification illustrates the different effects that local and global information access have on the evolution of majority opinion. Ask participants to consider how and why this change affects the rate at which the group comes to a consensus.

RUNNING THE ACTIVITY—EXTENSIONS

You can consider making some of the following modifications to this Activity:

- Rather than having people move about randomly during each stage, ask them to get into groups of a fixed size. Start with 2 or 3 people per group. Ask each group member to share their color choice with the other group members. Mix up the small groups after each tally. Try using larger group sizes. How does the size of the small group affect the rate at which the whole group reaches consensus?

- Ask participants to walk more slowly and veer to the right, so that they often interact with the same people. Do factors like speed and direction influence the dynamics of color choice?

- Whisper a new color like yellow or red to one group member. Does this color spread through the population?

- Instead of instructing people to choose a color, ask them to choose something that they feel more strongly about, such as their choice for mayor, their favorite car, or their favorite actor. When people feel more strongly about their choice, are they more or less likely to change their opinion?

- Change the rules of the game so that people are trying to be in the minority instead of the majority. How does this change affect the dynamics of color choice? What sorts of modifications do people make to their decision-making process?

FACTS FOR FACILITATORS

This Activity is a good opportunity for discussing the rules that people use when they make decisions. It also illustrates the difference between local and global access to information. In the first stage of this Activity, it is important to prevent people from purposely or accidentally communicating nonlocally. If people whisper too loudly, the dynamics can be changed dramatically. If you are concerned about the possibility of global information exchange, ask participants to discreetly show their Post-It notes to one another when they meet (instead of whispering).

In some groups it might be difficult to get "random" mixing of the entire group. Small cliques can form, altering the dynamics of the system. You can either make an effort to break up these groups or discuss the impact that reduced mixing has on the dynamics.

Many people have difficulty understanding the concept of sampling and how a poll of only a few hundred people can represent the opinions of millions. Ask participants how many people they needed to interact with before they felt confident about their color choice. Did the size of this sample change as they played the game again and again? Were they uncomfortable when you imposed a small sample size by demanding group counts in quick succession or dividing the participants into small groups? Discussing these effects can help people understand the nature of sampling.

While sometimes sampling accurately reflects the properties of the whole system, data can also be manipulated in ways that mask the true properties of the system. For some funny, engaging tales of the ways that people lie with numbers see Dewdney (1996) and Huff and Geis (1993).

The Plot Thickens

Often, interesting patterns emerge from the rules that the turtles follow in your StarLogo projects. Observing the evolution of these patterns can be captivating. But direct observation rarely provides reliable quantitative information about the whole turtle population. Your Challenge is to design and implement an innovative method to display turtle information. You might begin by creating a line graph, using the StarLogo **Plot Window** to visualize the changes in your model over time, or by using global monitors to keep track of aggregate information about your turtles. After exploring these built-in features, create your own graphic illustration using the turtles themselves to display information in a meaningful way.

In this Challenge, you can build your illustration in one of your own projects or a sample project. You can use the commands **setx** *position* and **sety** *position* to arrange the turtles.

Once you have created your graph, verify that the turtles are displaying information in the manner that you intended. One way to determine the accuracy of your illustration is to open up the **Turtle Monitors**. Can you figure out if all of the turtles are in the right place? What information is most clearly displayed in your graph? What information is missing? The projects *Disease* and *Reaction* show some new types of illustrations and allow you to restart the simulation after viewing an illustration by pressing the **go-back** and **go** buttons.

EXPLORATIONS

◆ Which type of graphic illustration allows you to make better predictions about the system?

◆ How do your graphs differ from StarLogo's built-in tools (global monitors and time series plots)? When are you likely to use the plotting tool? Your own graph? When is a global monitor useful?

◆ Can you think of other ways to implement turtle-based graphs? Perhaps you could ask the turtles to gather in circles that show their state. Or you could ask the turtles to line up using a different variable.

◆ Try modifying one aspect of the project that you are using. Can you see the effects of this change in your graph?

CHALLENGE PHILOSOPHY

Take just a few seconds to think about some data that you know well, like the statistics of your favorite basketball player, the local temperature for the past 10 days, or the price of a stock that you are following. Now spend a few moments visualizing your data. What did you picture? Experts in many fields find graphs immensely helpful for sorting out information, identifying trends, and predicting future results. Unfortunately, it often takes students a long time to learn how to interpret and create graphs, so they do not develop an appreciation of the importance of graphing.

As you model systems in StarLogo, you may notice that it can be difficult to discern exactly what is happening in your model. Is the number of turtles increasing or decreasing? Are there more yellow or blue turtles on the screen? Sometimes the turtles move so quickly that it is nearly impossible to see any pattern in their activity. Other times, you may have carefully chosen colors for turtles—each of which has a particular meaning—only to see all of those colors blur together as the turtles cluster.

This Challenge uses the turtles and two built-in StarLogo tools to help you see and interpret what is happening in your projects. You will design and build several different illustrations of the behavior in your models. The sample projects show how turtles can chart their own states, global monitors can display aggregate information, and time series plots can illustrate behavior over time.

CHALLENGE DESCRIPTION

In this Challenge, you will devise an innovative way to evaluate the dynamics of your model system. You could program the turtles to create a bar graph or a scatter plot. Or you could rank the turtles based on their states. Once you create an illustration, compare it to the two built-in tools for analyzing systems—time series plots and global monitors—as well as the turtle-based illustrations in the sample projects. How do the various illustrations help you to better understand your model?

The importance of any particular data set varies widely from person to person, so you can complete this Challenge by adding to one of the sample projects or by augmenting a project that you have already built. In **Disease**, an infection spreads through the turtle population. You can track the infection over time or see the distribution of diseased turtles as a function of their ages. The **Reaction** project models a system of two reversible chemical reactions. You can follow the concentrations of the chemicals in the system over time or look at their relative distributions at a single moment in time. You should explore several different ways to visualize quantitative data.

MODELING CONCEPTS

◆ Explore ways to illustrate the aggregate results of individual decision making.

◆ Compare different representations of the same data.

◆ Develop tools that help you make predictions about the behavior of a complex system.

STARLOGO CONCEPTS

◆ Use global monitors to gather quantitative information about a system.

◆ Create graphs using turtles.

◆ Construct plots that display time series data.

CHALLENGE GUIDELINES

In this Challenge, you will track data about the turtles. The sample projects incorporate several different techniques to gather information about the population of turtles. Your Challenge is to invent another illustration that uses the turtles themselves to display information about their states. Try to build illustrations that help you investigate the behavior of your model.

Disease

In this sample project, a disease afflicts the turtle population. Though most turtles start out healthy, many eventually succumb to the disease. When a turtle is infected, by sharing a patch with an infected turtle, it becomes a latent carrier of the disease. Soon it becomes sick and displays symptoms of the disease. Eventually, it recovers or dies. Recovered turtles are no longer susceptible to the disease.

Turtles contract the disease from other infected turtles with the probability specified by the infect-rate slider and recover with the probability specified by the recover-rate slider. Turtles remain latent for latent-time and sick for sick-time. You can specify the initial conditions of the simulation with the number and infected sliders.

Try exploring the effects of infect-rate and recover-rate while you run the simulation. How many turtles do you think are sick? Remember that you can double-click on any turtle to check on its variables, like **age** and **health**. How easy is it to assess and predict the effects of different rates?

Which turtles are more likely to be sick? To recover? Press stop-it and use the pop-dist button to create a distribution of turtles by **age**, with the youngest turtles on the left. The height of each line shows how many turtles fall into a particular age bracket. Open a few **Turtle Monitors** to see if all of the turtles are in the correct position. Does this distribution give you additional clues about the dynamics of the disease? You can restart the simulation by pressing start or by first asking the turtles to go-back to their previous positions and then pressing start. How do the dynamics of disease transmission change if you start without asking the turtles to go-back?

The Disease project and bar graph.

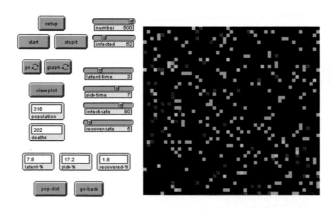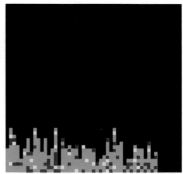

Reaction

Reaction employs five different turtle colors to simulate the following system of reversible chemical reactions:

	In English this reads:
Reaction 1: red + blue ⟷ yellow	Reaction 1: When a red turtle encounters a blue turtle, they combine to form a yellow turtle. Sometimes a yellow turtle decomposes into a red turtle and a blue turtle.
Reaction 2: yellow + white ⟷ green	Reaction 2: When a yellow turtle encounters a white turtle, they combine to form a green turtle. Sometimes a green turtle decomposes into a yellow turtle and a white turtle.

You can control the probability of the forward reactions using the reaction-1 and reaction-2 sliders. The probability of the reverse reactions is defined as 1 minus the probability of the forward reactions. Adjusting the temperature slider controls the speed of molecular movement. To change the initial conditions, simply reset the color sliders.

Can you observe the effects of different reaction rates on the system? Does a change in temperature alter the equilibrium or the dynamics of the system? How do changes in the initial conditions influence the equilibrium? Try investigating these parameters using the pie chart. Stop the simulation, and then click on the draw-piechart button to display the relative concentrations of the molecules. You can start the simulation again by pressing start or go-back and then start. Does the pie chart help you understand the reaction dynamics? The equilibrium concentrations?

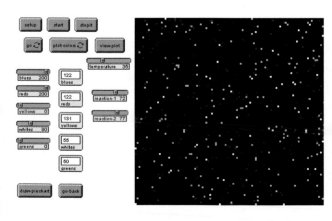
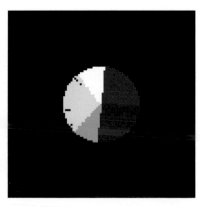

The Reaction project and a pie chart.

Global Monitors

Both sample projects use global monitors to display precise numerical data about the population of turtles. For example, *Disease* has a monitor that shows the percentage of latent, sick, and recovered turtles in the population. Look at the code for the sick-% monitor by Control double-clicking (or Shift double-clicking on a Mac) on the monitor. It calls the Observer Procedure sick-%, which reads as follows:

```
to sick-%
  output ((count-turtles-with [health = sick]) * 100) / count-turtles
end
```

This procedure uses the command output to return a value, which is then displayed in the monitor. Using the global monitors, are you better able to predict the outcome of a simulation?

Building Time Series Plots

In addition to the global monitors, the sample projects for this Challenge use StarLogo's built-in plot commands to display information about the turtle population over time. For instance, in *Reaction* you can track the concentration of each chemical over time by turning on the plot-colors button and opening the Plot Window.

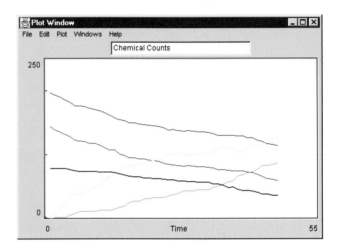

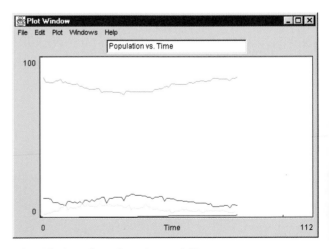

Plot Windows from Reaction and Disease.

You can create time series plots in any project using the Observer Commands on the following page.

If you want to...	Use these commands:	For this character:
Select which number pen you want to issue a command to	The command **ppnumber** (where *number* is the number of the pen that you are selecting) tells StarLogo the pen to which you are going to issue a command. This command is followed by another command, such as **plot** or **ppreset**.	
Clear the whole plot	The command **clear-plot** resets the plot window.	
Clear the plot made by one of the pens	The command **ppreset** clears the plot made by whichever pen is currently selected.	
Choose the color of a plotting pen	The command **setppc** *color* sets the color of whichever pen is currently selected to the *color* that is specified.	
Set the plotting range on the x or y axes	The commands **setplot-xrange** *minimum maximum* and **setplot-yrange** *minimum maximum* set the x- and y-plot ranges to the *minimum* and *maximum* values specified.	
Plot the current value of a variable as the y value and the current time step as the x value	The command **plot** *value* directs the selected pen to **plot** a point on the graph on the y-axis at the *value* specified and on the x-axis at the next available value. By default the points are connected by a line.	
Plot individual points	The command **ppu** (for **plot pen up**) causes the plot pen to draw x's instead of plotting a continuous line. Use **ppd** to switch back to a continuous line.	
Put a title on your plot	The command **setplot-title** *"name"* sets the plot title to *name* .	
Label the plot axes	The commands **setplot-xlabel** *"x-axis name"* and **setplot-ylabel** *"y-axis name"* allow you to put labels on the axes of your plot.	

CHALLENGE HINTS

TIPS FOR TEACHERS

Encourage your students to articulate how their illustrations help them understand what is going on in their projects. Illustrations of data can be invaluable tools as students design and run experiments with their models. Ask students to analyze how the utility of information can change based on the way that it is displayed.

While graphic illustrations can be powerful tools for analyzing data, your students may have trouble inventing their own designs. Encourage them to collect examples of some of the different methods that people use to illustrate data. The front page of *USA Today* is a great place to start. Can your students find any pie charts? Bar graphs? Histograms? Scatter plots? Ask them to replicate one of these techniques in their projects.

Some graphics are created out of geometric shapes, but there are instances in which illustrations are more reflective of the objects that they represent. For example, a designer might choose pictures of coins to represent financial information, drawings of people to show population data, or icons of small pills to illustrate pharmaceutical sales. Similarly, students can use turtles to form charts or graphs, as shown in **Disease** and **Reaction**. For an advanced look at the visual organization of data, see Tufte (1983, 1990, 1997).

Flight of the Humanboids

When people see a flock of birds flying or a school of fish swimming, they often assume that there must be a leader. When that same flock or school reacts to a predator in a strikingly coherent fashion—almost as if it were a single large organism—it seems even more likely that a leader is in charge of the group's movement. In fact, flocking patterns typically arise without a leader. Many other patterns in nature arise in the same way, through decentralized interactions among individual animals.

As swallows dart through the sky, they often fly in a tight formation. Yet, you never see two swallows crash into one another. During the flight, each bird follows a set of rules designed to maintain an appropriate distance from the other birds. They want to be close to the other birds, but not too close. By transforming participants into bird-like creatures called "humanboids," this Activity demonstrates how coordinated behaviors can develop from simple rules that each member of a group follows. In order to form a flock, the humanboids will need to determine a suitable set of flocking rules.

MODELING CONCEPTS

◆ Create patterns without relying on centralized control.

◆ Design and test some flocking rules.

◆ Learn how flocks can adapt to changing environmental conditions.

MATERIALS

◆ A large open space

◆ A place to record the rules

RUNNING THE ACTIVITY

Ask the group to determine a set of flocking rules. These rules might contain instructions specifying what to do if you get too far from other humanboids, how to avoid collisions, or how to respond to obstacles. You might suggest that participants consider the attributes of a flock, like spacing, speed, heading, and so forth. Write the rules down on paper. This process helps disambiguate the rules and ensures that everyone in the group has agreed on each of the rules. Note: It is possible to come up with hundreds of rules to control flocking behavior. Remind the humanboids that they will need to follow these rules, so it is best to agree on a few general rules that everyone can remember and execute.

When a set of rules is established, send your flock to a large open space (preferably a gymnasium or an outdoor space) and ask them to fly. There should be no verbal communication between humanboids while they are flocking. Let the flock run for several minutes. Did the rules work right away? Did they break down (or begin to work) over time?

Regroup the flock so that they can discuss their flocking behavior. They might want to consider the following questions:

- Were the rules adequate to generate flocking behavior or was there improvisation during the Activity?

- Which rules were most important or effective in forming the flock? Is there anything special about these rules?

- Did one or more people take a leadership role? How did this affect the implementation of the rules?

- Would the rules be adequate to avoid a stationary obstacle? How about a predator?

- What would happen to their flock if one humanboid suddenly dropped out?

Ask the group to come up with a revised set of flocking rules and return to an open space to fly. Did the new or additional rules prove to be more effective? The group might want to try some advanced flocking behavior such as predator or obstacle avoidance or the formation of specific patterns (V shapes, wide or narrow groups, etc.). What kinds of rules are needed to achieve these kinds of flocking behaviors?

FACTS FOR FACILITATORS

The humanboids might initially have a hard time forming coherent flocks. Encourage members of the group to revise their flocking rules if they think this will improve the formation. (But try to do this as a group, rather than allowing a dispersed flock to fly while individual humanboids spontaneously alter their behavior.) It can take several iterations to create a recognizable flock.

In other cases, participants succeed in forming a flock, but only by "cheating" (even if they aren't aware of it). Rather than rigorously following the rules they agreed upon, they might improvise on the fly. You should emphasize the importance of sticking precisely to the agreed-upon rules.

Sometimes, the difficulty of decentralized flock formation leads the humanboids to conclude that flocks cannot form without a leader. If this situation occurs, encourage them to consider alternative explanations. How carefully and consistently were they following their flocking rules? Do they believe that their rules were sufficient to form a flock? (How could they test this belief?) What new rules would they add to improve their flocking behavior? The lives of some birds depend on their flocking ability. These birds must follow good flocking rules or risk death. Could participants devise and follow a more effective set of flocking rules if there were negative consequences for straying from the flock? To simulate these consequences, you can "prey on" straying humanboids by removing them from the flock.

You might discuss how flocking rules originated. Does each group of birds have a fixed set of flocking rules, like the humanboids did? Or do the rules evolve over time?

Craig Reynolds is the original creator of computerized birdlike objects, called "boids." His boids model coordinated animal motion such as bird flocks and fish schools. See http://www.red3d.com/cwr/boids for more information. For related activities check out Schools are for Fish at http://www.meas.ncsu.edu/outreach/fish_school.html.

How to Track a Turtle

Do you feel as if you have been wandering around aimlessly? Have you been traveling across patches with no particular destination? Do you wish that you could gain some direction? Well, look no further! You can get the direction you desire from a command that lets you head towards any other turtle, as long as you know its **who** number. That versatile command is:

seth towards xcor-of *whonumber*
ycor-of *whonumber*

This command sets the **heading** of the turtles in the direction of the turtle *whonumber*.

Now that you know the secret to finding some direction, build a project in which turtles head towards a moving target (another turtle). You might want to build this behavior into one of your previous projects or try starting with one of these ideas:

EXPLORATIONS

POSSIBLE

◆ Notice that in the sample project *Gotya* it is difficult to count the number of "tagged" turtles. Modify the project so that the last tagged turtle chases the turtle who was tagged immediately before it.

◆ Try building a project in which a shy turtle heads *away from* the paparazzi.

◆ Create a turtle who grabs a **partner** and then heads towards it. When the turtle reaches its **partner**, instruct it to drop that **partner** and select a new one. Does your model remind you of any real-world systems?

• Build a game of Tag in which the "it" chooses and seeks out its next target.

• Create a model of a pickpocket on a crowded city square.

• Build a model of a lion hunting a zebra.

CHALLENGE PHILOSOPHY

A great diversity of behaviors can arise from simple rules that you write. But sometimes, augmenting those simple rules can lead to a more realistic model. Many of the objects and creatures in your earlier simulations headed in particular directions but did not possess the ability to set their course towards specific destinations. You can endow your creatures with the ability to chart their own course by giving them the means to track other objects in the environment. Just as male birds chase female birds in order to initiate mating rituals and bees keep track of the location of their hive so that they can return to it after foraging for food, your creatures can follow or find other objects and creatures in their environment. Incorporating behaviors like these into your own simulations broadens the range of behaviors that you can simulate and enables you to investigate sophisticated interactions in complex systems.

You are becoming an experienced model builder and are developing an appreciation for why researchers use simulation tools. Simulation environments enable people to conduct highly iterative experiments, represent data in a variety of ways, and model behaviors that capture elements of real-world behaviors. In order to engage in productive analyses of simulations, it is best if your models incorporate only the most salient features of the system. As you design creatures with behaviors that are analogous to real-world behaviors, be sure to keep the goals of your model in mind. Don't let the complexity of your model obscure the very dynamics that you want to study.

MODELING CONCEPTS

◆ Explore ways to apply chasing, tracking, and following behaviors.

◆ Tackle problems associated with maintaining appropriate, relative speeds when one creature is tracking another.

CHALLENGE DESCRIPTION

In this Challenge, you will give turtles the ability to head towards other turtles. This behavior is demonstrated in a simple game of Tag that shows "tagged" turtles following a leader turtle. The "heading-towards" behavior that the tagged turtles employ can be used in many different scenarios. You might approach this Challenge with lingering ideas from previous explorations. Since the code required to produce the heading-towards behavior is modular, this approach should work just fine. Alternatively, you might try to conceive an entirely new project idea that incorporates heading towards. Deciding which kinds of project ideas to pursue is highly dependent on your own specific goals.

CHALLENGE GUIDELINES

The procedure for instructing a turtle to follow another turtle is based on several new concepts. The command **seth towards** *x-coordinate* *y-coordinate* provides the basic framework for making a turtle head in a particular direction, towards the point specified by *x-coordinate* and *y-coordinate*. For example, the command **seth towards 0 0** would make a turtle head towards the center of the screen (which is at location 0, 0).

STARLOGO CONCEPTS

◆ Discover new ways that turtles can interact with each other.

◆ Learn how a turtle can move towards another turtle or location.

◆ Interact directly with the turtles.

If you want a turtle to head towards another turtle, you need to find out the location of the other turtle: You can use **xcor-of** *whonumber* to get the x-coordinate of the turtle and **ycor-of** *whonumber* to get the y-coordinate. Putting these concepts together results in the command:

seth towards (xcor-of *whonumber***) (ycor-of** *whonumber***)**

which sets the **heading** of a turtle **towards** the turtle with the specified *whonumber*. One use of this command is demonstrated in the sample project **Gotya**.

Gotya

This project shows a clever way of using heading towards. The turtles in **Gotya** play a version of Tag in which the first turtle (**who** number 0) is "it." The "it" turtle (white) and the pool of "taggable" turtles (green) run randomly around the screen. If the "it" turtle lands on an untagged turtle, "it" tags the other turtle by turning it red. When the appropriate switch is thrown, the tagged turtles follow the "it" turtle.

Gotya's Interface.

Click the setup button to create the number of turtles indicated on the numturts slider. One of those turtles is designated as "it" and colored white, while the others are untagged, green turtles. Instead of relying on numeric values to indicate a turtle's **caught** state in **Gotya**, the words **yes**, **no**, and **it** are used instead.

When you click go, the turtles move randomly about the screen. It is captivating to watch the turtles move apart and back together as you toggle the together slider. Observing this process is a good way to get a feel for how turtles head towards other turtles. As you are reading through the code, be sure to look at the line **seth towards xcor-of 0 ycor-of 0**, which is the command that makes red turtles head towards the "it" turtle (whose **who** number is zero).

The interface for this project employs a true/false slider to regulate the tagged turtles' following behavior. As turtles get tagged, they follow "it" if the together slider is toggled to 1, and they move randomly if the slider is toggled to 0. The count-tagged monitor keeps track of the total number of turtles who have been tagged, which is useful when the tagged turtles are bunched up behind "it." Finally, the slow button (which is scaled by the time slider) can be used to slow down the whole process if you'd like to watch the game more carefully.

Gotya's Graphics Canvas over time.

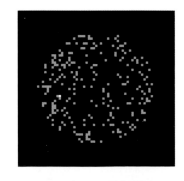
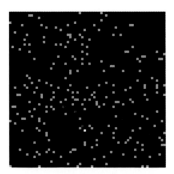

Mouse Commands

You already know that turtles can follow other turtles, but you might not know that turtles can also follow mice—computer mice, that is. Turtles can locate the mouse on the **Graphics Canvas** and can even tell whether the mouse button is down. Using this information, the turtles can follow the mouse around the screen or run a command when you click the mouse button. Both the turtles and the observer can use the following mouse commands:

If you want to...	Use these commands:	For this character:
Find the coordinates of the current mouse location	The commands **mouse-xcor** and **mouse-ycor** return the x-coordinate and y-coordinate of the mouse as long as it is on the **Graphics Canvas**. For example the Turtle Command, **seth towards mouse-xcor mouse y-cor** points turtles **towards** the current mouse location.	
Find out whether the mouse button is pressed	The command **mouse-down?** returns true if the mouse button is down and false if it is not.	

TIPS FOR TEACHERS

Spatially directed behavior dramatically influences the dynamics of many systems. Even in inanimate systems, directed movement can create patterns in the system. Picture a tray filled with iron filings. If you shake the tray, then the filings will move around, but the overall pattern of evenly distributed filings will remain. But if you place a strong magnet over the center of the tray, then a large tower of filings will grow up to the magnet. Though directed movement is powerful, it is not the only source of interesting patterns and dynamics.

Now that your students know how to program heading towards, make sure that they still appreciate the important role that random movement plays in systems. You might remind them of the story of the fireflies. If you catch some fireflies in a glass jar and hold the jar with the open end pointed away from a strong light, the fireflies will head towards the light instead of escaping through the opening. Luckily, sometimes the fireflies move with a bit of randomness and by chance they will eventually fly out of the jar. Without any random movement, the fireflies would perish. It is the combination of directed and random movement that enables fireflies to survive. Mathematicians and economists commonly study problems like this one as part of optimization theory. You can find examples of both random and directed movement in projects such as *Slime* and *King of the Hill*. Unlike the turtles in *Gotya*, the turtles in these two projects head towards specific features in their environment rather than towards other turtles.

Graphics Canvases from King of the Hill and Slime.

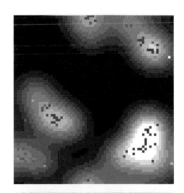

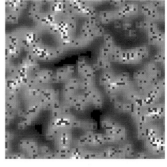

ACTIVITY 10

The Gambler's Dilemma

When observing the behavior of a group, you might notice that the aggregate dynamics frequently differ from what you might expect based on the sum or average of all of the individual decisions. Imagine a pack of wolves or a pride of lions hunting for food. During the hunt, the individuals in the group interact with each other in a way that enables them to capture an animal that no single one of them could successfully kill alone. The activity of the pack or the pride is different from the movement of any individual animal. In fact, their coordinated behavior extends beyond the hunt. A felled prey is not eaten solely by the capturing predator—instead, it is distributed among the group of predators that worked together to kill it.

The results of acting alone (e.g., hunting individually) are vastly different from the results of all of the group members acting in a cooperative manner. Without cooperation, no individual group member can secure the necessary resources. Similarly, the consequences of individuals acting selfishly (e.g., single-handedly eating the whole prey) have grave ramifications for the group. Though one individual may secure great resource gains, the group as a whole suffers. Without cooperation, the costs and benefits for the individual do not mirror the costs and benefits for the group. Cooperative behavior can lead to the fate of the individual members mirroring the fate of the group.

The Gambler's Dilemma enables direct exploration of the development of group processes that are based on individually determined actions and threatened by selfish behavior. During this Activity, individuals make decisions about strategies to acquire money. Cooperative behavior by everyone results in a small financial gain for each group member, while selfish behavior can result in a large gain for a single individual or no gain for anyone. The trade-offs between individual and group costs and benefits create a rich setting for exploring group dynamics.

RUNNING THE ACTIVITY—PART 1

To start this game, you (the financier) should give every player a Post-It note and a small amount of money—either one or five dollars depending on the size of the group and your gambling tendencies (see Facts for Facilitators). Make sure that the group is absolutely silent from the moment you begin distributing the money. When everyone has received their money, describe the following rules:

❶ If every member of the group decides to "cooperate," then everyone keeps the money they received.

❷ If one and *only one* person "defects," then that person gets to keep all of the money from the whole group.

❸ If more than one person "defects," then all of the money is returned to you.

Tell each player to write down on the Post-It note whether he or she is going to "cooperate" or "defect." There should be no discussion among the players, and no player should see anyone else's note. When the players have settled on a strategy, ask them to stand on their notes. When everyone has made their decisions, ask the "defectors" to raise their hands. What happened? Are people surprised? Upset? Why? Regardless of the outcome, consider the following questions with the group:

- Why did the defector(s) choose to defect?

- Why did the cooperator(s) choose to cooperate?

- What were the costs and benefits that people considered in their decisions?

- Did they consider their options from an individual or a group perspective?

- How did they weigh financial costs and benefits versus other less tangible costs and benefits (e.g., potential shame associated with defecting)?

- Can they think of any real-world analogs to this game? Do their actions make sense in the context of the real-world analogs they describe?

MODELING CONCEPTS

◆ Explore the factors involved in decision making.

◆ Investigate the balance between optimal individual strategies and successful group strategies.

MATERIALS

◆ Either a one-dollar or five-dollar bill per participant

◆ Post-It notes or small pieces of paper

You can choose to run a second version of the same game, this time allowing group discussion during strategy formation. It is a good idea to impose a time limit of two or three minutes on this discussion. Often some members of the group attempt to convince players to adopt strategies that could potentially benefit everyone. Surprisingly, group discussion does not always change the outcome of the game, since there is still money to be won by acting selfishly. The outcome of this second game raises some additional questions including:

- Did leaders emerge during the discussion? If so, how were they chosen? Were their strategies eventually adopted?

- Did the group reach a consensus? If so, how was the group decision made?

- Were participants comfortable with this method, or did they feel it stripped them of their personal freedom?

- Did new costs and benefits enter into this round of decision making?

- Were participants influenced by what happened in the previous game?

At this point, you might want to extend the discussion to consider real-world systems in which stable communities cooperate over extended periods of time. What other social pressures serve to regulate behavior in these communities? What do the participants in the Gambler's Dilemma think might have happened if you had allowed them to play for an unlimited number of games? How might participants modify their strategies? How might these modifications change the outcome for the group? Would their strategies have differed if they played with a select group of good friends? What if they played with people they had never met before?

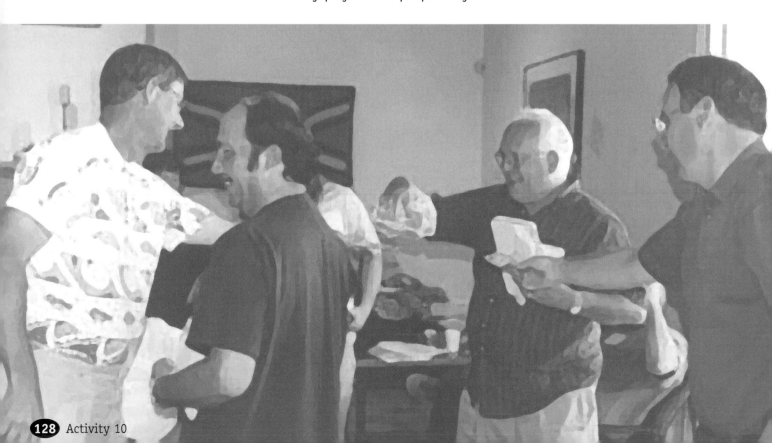

Finally, you might play, or consider what it would be like to play, the same game with different payoff structures. For example, suppose that individuals received less money for selfish behavior and more for cooperative behavior. What if you allow two or three defectors to split the pot of money? What other payoff structures would be interesting to consider? Does changing the amount of money at stake change people's strategies?

FACTS FOR FACILITATORS

It is unlikely, but not inconceivable, that all of the players will cooperate or only one player will defect. This means that there is a small but measurable chance that you, the financier, will have to part with the money you provided. Be sure to consider this chance when deciding how much money is at stake. You might also consider alternative commodities such as candy. If you decide to use an alternative "currency" or decide not to play the game for "keeps," then consider the impact that this decision will have on the players' cost and benefit analyses.

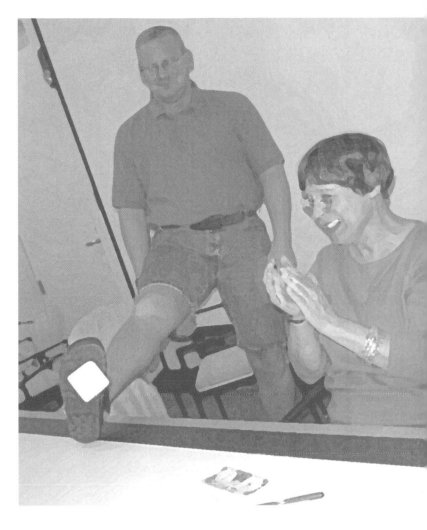

It is important to keep the players honest. Make sure that they write their strategies down in a way that other players cannot see and that cannot be altered during the latter stages of the game.

This Activity is derived from the classic problem of the Prisoner's Dilemma. For more information see Axelrod (1984) and Schelling (1978). For further explorations of this topic check out **http://www.taumoda.com/web/PD/setup.html**. This site provides a tutorial and interactive modeling activities related to this problem.

Breeds—The Final Frontier

Until now you have been addressing all of the individuals in your projects as turtles. You can use **breeds** of turtles to give different groups of turtles their own unique behaviors. Your Challenge is to create a project in which different kinds of turtles interact with one another in ways that reflect their identities. Use the Turtle Commands **one-of-*breeds*-here** and **if breed = *breed1* [*statements*]** as well as the Observer Command **ask-*breed1* [*statements*]** to direct groups of turtles in your project.

For instance, you could build:

• A demonstration of how electrons and protons join to form neutrons.

• A model of a high school dance. (With whom will you dance? On what will you base your decisions?)

• A simulation that illustrates how people's political opinions can be influenced by others.

• A model of a lion killing a zebra. (Note: This is a bit more difficult than just chasing the zebra.) Can you build a more complex ecosystem now?

EXPLORATIONS

POSSIBLE

◆ Brainstorm a list of possible topics for new StarLogo projects.

◆ Now that you have completed all of the Challenges, you are in the top echelon of StarLogo scholars. Try to integrate many of the concepts that you have covered and apply them to a system that interests you. Think about what you might want to learn from creating a model of your system, and what kinds of questions might arise from that model. Let these ideas guide your creation of many more StarLogo models.

CHALLENGE PHILOSOPHY

Imagine that you have created a population of cats. The cats in your model might chase Ping-Pong balls around the room, groom one another, or lounge in sunny spots. Perhaps they even search for small, edible creatures. However, if you introduced mice into your model, you would want the mice to possess their own set of unique behaviors. The mice might eat cheese, sleep in a big pile, and scamper under furniture. In addition to these "species-specific" behaviors, you would probably want to add ways for the cats and mice to interact.

While there are many ways to classify objects in the world (by color, shape, or size), it is often useful to separate objects by their behaviors. This Challenge helps you create models in which classes of turtles behave in unique ways. In the past, you might have defined different sets of behavior using **color** or another variable to distinguish between groups of turtles. For instance:

> **if color = red [setspeed red-speed]**
> **if color = blue [setspeed blue-speed]**

In this case, a straightforward **if** statement ensures that only certain turtles—red ones or blue ones—listen to a set of commands.

However, in some instances, distinguishing turtles by **color** or another turtle variable is not sufficient to implement a model. Perhaps you want mice to behave differently when they run into cats than when they run into mice, but you want to use **color** to indicate age.

CHALLENGE DESCRIPTION

This Challenge introduces the concept of **breeds**, which is a powerful and flexible means of distinguishing groups of turtles. Here you will see three examples that use **breeds** to differentiate among groups of turtles. These sample projects illustrate the use of breeds to define different behaviors for classes of turtles (e.g., mice behaving like mice and cats behaving like cats). You can create a project that uses **breeds** to define different kinds of behaviors or that mediates different kinds of interactions between turtles (e.g., how the cats and mice interact with each other). This second use of **breeds** is more complex and will draw upon your knowledge from previous Challenges.

MODELING CONCEPTS

- ◆ Define categories (**breeds**) of individuals in a model.

- ◆ Instruct some classes (**breeds**) to behave differently than others.

- ◆ Specify interactions based on individual classification.

STARLOGO CONCEPTS

- ◆ Learn how to implement **breeds**.

- ◆ Ask one kind of turtle to treat other kinds of turtles differently.

- ◆ Complete the final StarLogo Challenge!

CHALLENGE GUIDELINES

Creating Breeds

Creating new **breeds** is as easy as creating new turtle variables. In fact, you can think of **breeds** as a special kind of turtle variable. If you open a Turtle Monitor, you will see **breed** in addition to **color**, **heading**, and so forth. If you have not created a **breed** yet, you will see that **breed** is set to zero. To create **breeds**, type **breeds** [*breed1 breed2*] at the very top of the **Turtle Procedures Pane** . In this statement *breed1* and *breed2* are sample breed names. You should make sure that you put all of the **breeds** on a single line and only type the **breeds** command once in any project. For instance, if you wanted to create the **breeds lions** and **tigers** and **bears**, you would type:

> **breeds [lions tigers bears]**

Notice that, like turtle variables, there are no commas between the **breeds** and that you must put the **breeds** in between one set of square brackets.

Once you have created **breeds**, you will probably want to create some turtles of each breed type. To create and use turtles of particular **breeds**, you will need to use some new commands.

If you want to...	Use these commands:	For this character:
Create a new breed for all turtles	The statement **breeds** [*breedname*] creates a new breed *breedname*, and allows you to use a special set of commands to address only *breedname*. Try: **breeds [lions]**.	This statement should be placed at the top of the **Turtle Procedures Pane**.
Create turtles of a particular breed	The command **create-***breed1 number* creates the number of turtles of type *breed1* specified by *number*. For example, to create 12 turtles of type lions you would use the command **create-lions 12**.	
Change a turtle from one breed to another	Use the command **setbreed** *breed2* to change an existing turtle from its current breed to *breed2*.	
Ask all lions to do something	The command **if breed = lions** [*statements*] instructs all of the **lions** to perform the *statements*.	
	The command **ask-lions** [*statements*] instructs all of the **lions** to perform the *statements*.	
Count the number of turtles in a breed	The command **count-***breed1* returns the number of *breed1* turtles alive at that moment and can be used with any breed that you have created.	

CHALLENGE HINTS

There are many other useful commands that are made available in StarLogo every time a new breed is created. Many of the commands that have the word turtles in them can be applied to a specific breed by using the name of the breed instead of the word turtles. For a complete list of breed-related commands, see the StarLogo Documentation at **http://www.media.mit.edu/starlogo/documentation/breeds.htm**.

A Sample Use of Breeds

In this Challenge, you will instruct breeds of turtles to interact with one another based upon which type (breed) of turtle they encounter. Imagine you have two kinds of turtles: Purple turtles and orange turtles. The purple turtles represent mice and the orange turtles represent cats. Think about how you might create a model in which the cats interact differently with mice than they do with other cats. Your cats will need to know when they encounter a mouse.

Recall the command one-of-turtles-here. That command allows a turtle to look at the patch that it is on and interact with another turtle on the same patch (here). Imagine a whole stack of turtles, some that are purple and some that are orange. What if you wanted a orange turtle to pick a purple turtle with which to interact?

The Turtle Command one-of-turtles-here returns the who of one of the turtles on the patch. So the code
  if color = orange [setprey one-of-turtles-here]
instructs the orange turtles (cats) to set their prey variable to the who of one of the turtles on their patch.

Remember, however, that your task was to instruct a "cat" turtle to interact with a "mouse" turtle. The orange turtle needs to make sure that the one-of-turtles-here command returns a who from a purple turtle. But, there is no command one-of-turtles-here-with [color = purple].

You can solve this dilemma using breeds. Start by creating two breeds, cats and mice, and a turtle variable for prey as follows:

  breeds [cats mice]
  turtles-own [prey]

You can now ask the cats to set their sights on a mouse like this:
  if breed = cats [setprey one-of-mice-here]

By using the command one-of-mice-here, you know that the cats will only record the who of one of the mice. Once the cat has selected a particular mouse as prey, you will have to tell it what to do with the mouse.

The following three sample projects use breeds to differentiate behavior among turtles. However, only the last project uses the breeds to mediate different kinds of interactions.

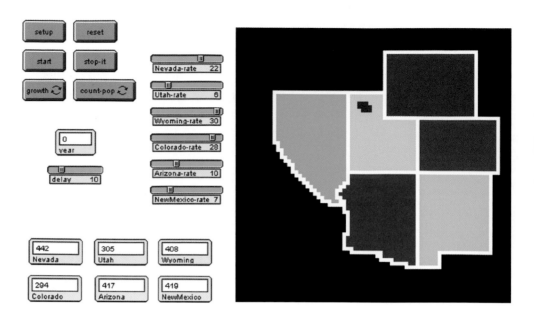

The Turtle Demographics project.

Turtle Demographics

Turtle Demographics models the human population explosion. setup is used to establish initial populations, and go starts the simulation. The sliders, Nevada-rate, Utah-rate, and so forth, control the birth rates for the different states. You can watch the populations grow on the **Graphics Canvas**, and you can track the actual populations in the monitors and in the **Plot Window**.

Breeds enable both the project and the user to distinguish between people in the various states. The different growth rates in the states mean that the turtles must know when to reproduce based on the growth rate for their state. Look at the **go** procedure. Notice that the turtles with **breed = nv** are following a different procedure than turtles with **breed = ut**. Turtles in each state reproduce when their breed is called upon to do so.

When using this model, note that, like all models, it is only as good as the assumptions that go into it. The assumptions in ***Turtle Demographics*** include a starting value for the growth rates of the states, the initial populations, and spatial constraints on population growth. Do the growth patterns look reasonable? Explore the difference that a slight change in growth rates or initial populations can have on the overall growth in the regions. What implications do these differences have for making predictions based on this model?

Traffic

This project models cars and trucks driving on a highway and swans swimming in a nearby river. Use the buttons setup, go, and stop-it to control the simulation. number controls the initial number of cars on the road. (You will have to setup the simulation again for a change in this slider to take effect.) lookahead controls how many spaces ahead each car looks to see if there is open driving room, and speedup and slowdown control the rates for acceleration and deceleration.

In this project there are four breeds:

breeds [lefts rights swans police]

If you look through the code, you will see that the swimming turtles have breed = swans and the driving turtles in the top lane have breed = lefts (similarly, those in the bottom lane have breed = rights). This project uses breeds to give different behaviors to different groups of turtles.

This project introduces a new way to ask turtles to perform tasks based on their breed. Earlier, you saw code that addressed breeds using an if statement such as:

if breed = swans [swim-in-the-river]

This project uses a different way of addressing breeds:

ask-swans [swim-in-the-river]

Both of these lines of code mean "if you are a turtle and your breed is swans, go swim-in-the-river." The difference between the two statements is that the command if breed = swans [swim-in-the-river] can only be executed by the turtles, while the command ask-swans [swim-in-the-river] can only be executed by the observer .

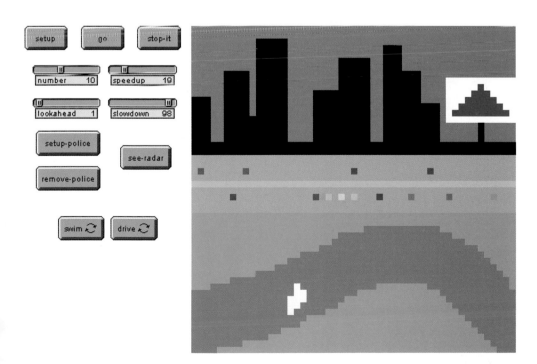

The Traffic project.

Similarly, **ask-lefts [drive-to-the-left]** (an Observer Command) ensures that only a subset of the cars on the screen will drive to the left. Notice that **ask-lefts** (just like **if breed = lefts**) requires that the set of instructions for the **lefts** be placed in between square brackets.

The cars in the traffic model follow three very simple rules:

❶ If there is a car ahead, then slow down.

❷ If there is no car ahead, then speed up.

❸ If you see a radar trap, then slow down.

While playing with the traffic model, you might notice that traffic jams can occur even when there is no radar trap. This model is an example of an emergent system. There is no centralized object that causes the traffic jam to form—it emerges out of the interactions of the cars. To see the effect of a police radar trap, use the setup-police button. The radar is visible to the turtles, but invisible to you unless you click on the see-radar button. By switching the radar trap on and off, you can compare the traffic patterns under two different conditions.

Predators, Prey, and Grass (Oh My!)

This project models an ecosystem consisting of growing grass, grasshoppers that eat the grass, and predators that eat the grasshoppers. The grasshoppers and predators are implemented as breeds of turtles, while the grass is implemented as patches.

If grass is present on a patch (with its density indicated by shades of green) it grows according to the rate specified in the solar-gain slider. Patches that have no grass at all are considered desertified and are shown in yellow. The only way grass can grow in the desertified areas is if it spreads to these patches through diffusion (one algorithm for modeling the reseeding of the desert patches).

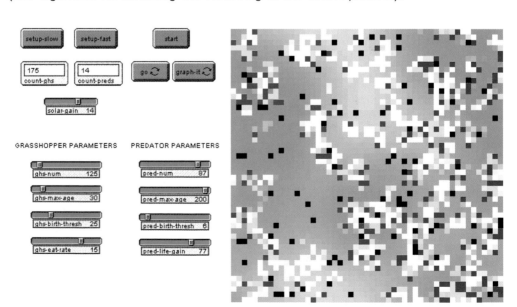

The Predators, Prey, and Grass project.

You control the initial number of grasshoppers with the ghs-num slider. Each grasshopper is created with an energy level. The grasshoppers move randomly around, using up a small amount of energy for each step. If a grasshopper lands on a green patch, it consumes the grass at a rate determined by the ghs-eat-rate slider. This rate determines both the amount of grass that the grasshopper eats and the amount of energy the grasshopper gains. If a grasshopper is over age 2 and has accumulated enough energy (as determined by the ghs-birth-thresh slider), then it will hatch a new grasshopper. If a grasshopper reaches the age shown on the ghs-max-age slider or runs out of energy, then it will die.

The pred-num slider sets the initial number of predators. These predators also have an energy level that decreases slightly as they move randomly around. If a predator encounters a grasshopper, then it will eat it and gain the amount of energy indicated on the pred-life-gain slider. Once a predator accumulates enough energy (as shown on the pred-birth-thresh slider), it will hatch a new predator. A predator dies when it runs out of energy or reaches the age shown on the pred-max-age slider.

Try running the model with the default parameters. What happens to the populations over time? Can you control the degree of population fluctuation? How? What seems to determine the degree of fluctuation? Try freezing all but one of the parameters and experimenting with different values for the remaining parameter. What happens to the populations of the three species as you change the parameter?

TIPS FOR TEACHERS

Congratulations on completing your first StarLogo Adventure! We hope that you and your students enjoyed your experiences along the way. We would like to encourage you to share your experiences with others. Please share any exemplary student work through the StarLogo Design Discussion Area at **http://education.mit.edu/starlogo/dda**. If you are willing to share your curriculum materials with other teachers, please contact us at **starlogo-adventures@media.mit.edu** so that we can arrange to put your work online. Also let us know if you are interested in running your own StarLogo workshop. Most of all we hope that this Adventure has inspired you to continue designing, creating, and investigating models.

A StarLogo Modeler Is Born

Open the project *Painted Turtles.* Can you use StarLogo's turtles to create patterns? What happens to your pattern if you create only one turtle? Two turtles? Twenty turtles?

Are your favorite patterns symmetrical or asymmetrical? Do your favorite patterns have common color schemes? Do you prefer patterns that are dynamic or static?

Try to design your own pattern using a sequence of buttons. What happens to the pattern if you execute the steps in a different order?

Opening StarLogo

Open StarLogo and go to the **File** menu and **Open Project...** Choose the file *Painted Turtles* inside the folder called Adventures Projects. Challenge 1 uses this project as the basis for your explorations.

EXPLORATIONS

POSSIBLE

◆ Try varying the initial number of turtles or their starting configurations to create graphic designs using the pattern buttons. For example, click the **create-flower** button followed by the **pattern-1** button or the **pattern-2** button.

◆ Try pressing different combinations of pattern buttons or running more than one button simultaneously. Now vary these patterns by repeating them while the turtles have their pens up or down. You can further vary the patterns by resetting the turtles' colors, using the **change-color** button.

◆ When you feel comfortable with the above explorations, try to create some cool graphics for yourself.

Painted Turtles

The buttons next to the **Graphics Canvas** are divided into three different categories ❶.
The first category is **Basic Commands** ❷. The buttons and sliders in this category
perform simple StarLogo commands. The function of each button and slider is as
described in the top section of the table below. The second category is **Setup Patterns**.
The buttons and sliders in this category arrange the turtles in more complex
configurations. The function of each button and slider is described in the bottom
section of the table below. The third category is **Action**. The five buttons in this
category move the turtles according to collections of simple commands called procedures. You can experiment with these buttons to learn more about what they do.

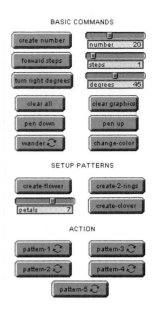

Painted Turtles' Interface.

For example, you can try the following exploration:

❶ Press the **clear all** button to begin.

❷ Create 20 turtles by setting the **number** slider to 20 and then pressing the
create number button.

❸ Put the turtles' pens down using the **pen down** button.

❹ Press the **pattern-1** button.

Try combining the patterns from the **Action** category with some of the buttons in
the **Basic Commands** category.

Basic Commands Buttons	Function
create number	Creates the number of turtles indicated by the slider **number**
forward steps	Moves each of the turtles forward the number of steps indicated by the slider **steps**
turn right degrees	Rotates each turtle clockwise by the number of degrees indicated by the slider **degrees**
clear all	Removes all graphics and kills all turtles
clear graphics	Removes all graphics
pen down	Tells all of the turtles to put their pens down
pen up	Tells all of the turtles to pick their pens up
wander (a **Forever** button indicated by the curved arrows to the right of "wander")	Moves and turns the turtles—like all **Forever** buttons, this button will stay depressed and continue running until you press it again to turn it off
change-color	Randomly changes the turtles' colors
Setup Patterns Buttons	Function
create-flower	Creates turtles in a flower shape with the number of petals indicated by the slider **petals**
create-2-rings	Creates two concentric circles of turtles
create-clover	Creates a clover-like shape made of turtles

Turtles, I Command Thee

Open the project *Return of the Painted Turtles*. In the **Custom Buttons** section, add your own buttons and sliders to control the turtle activity.

What kinds of patterns can you create by adding your own simple commands? What sorts of behavior can you generate using a series of commands? Can you build buttons that faithfully reproduce your favorite patterns by repeating a sequence of steps? What is the simplest set of commands you can use to create a complex pattern? Can you use the **Paint Tools** to set up different initial conditions?

Remember that StarLogo is a parallel language, so any command that you write for one turtle will be run by all of the turtles. When you issue any turtle instructions, *all* of the turtles will follow those commands.

EXPLORATIONS

POSSIBLE

◆ Try using the **repeat** command in conjunction with a slider that specifies the number of repetitions. Explore how varying the number of repetitions affects turtle behavior and the resulting pattern.

◆ Try to create buttons that make the turtles draw different shapes. What pattern emerges when 100 turtles each draw a triangle? You might use a slider to change the size of the shapes.

◆ See if you can make the turtles "wiggle" by making them repeatedly walk and turn.

Creating Buttons

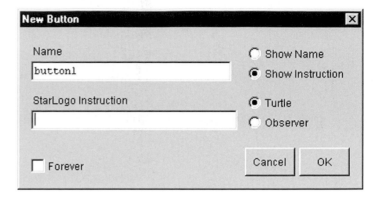

A button editor.

To create a new button:

❶ Click on the blue button icon in the **Toolbar**.

❷ In the **Interface** area, click and hold where you want to place the button. Drag the mouse down and to the right until you get to where you want to place the lower right-hand corner (you will see a rectangle the size of your new button). Release the mouse button.

❸ A button editor for the new button will pop up **❸**. Fill out the information for your button. If you'd like, you can name the button and click in the **Show Name** radio button. If you want the button to operate continuously, you should click the **Forever** check box. Finally, you should add the commands that you want the button to execute by typing them into the **StarLogo Instruction** field (you can type many commands in a row within a single button). Be sure that you check whether the **StarLogo Instructions** are for the turtles or the observer. Refer to the hints below for more information on specific actions that you can program into your buttons and the difference between Turtle and Observer Commands **❹**.

❹ Click **OK**.

Action	Process
Modify the contents of a button	Click the button icon on the **Main Toolbar**. Next, click on the button you want to change. Inside the button editor, you can change the button name and instructions, decide whether to show the name or instructions, mark whether the instructions are for the turtles or the observer, and choose if the button should run continuously (check **Forever**).
Delete a button	Press **Control** (or **Shift** on a Macintosh) and click on the button once, so that the little square handles appear. Press the **Delete** key.
Resize a button	Press **Control** (or **Shift** on a Macintosh) and click on the button once, so that the little square handles appear. To resize the button, click and hold the mouse button down while dragging one of the handles until the button is the desired size.
Move a button	Press **Control** (or **Shift** on a Macintosh) and click on the button once, so that the little square handles appear. Drag the button to the desired location.

As mentioned in Step 3, in order for the button to do something you will need to enter some commands in the **StarLogo Instruction** field of the button editor. The following hints will help you get started. Try using the commands in your buttons 🍎.

If you want to...	Use these commands:	For this character:

CHALLENGE HINTS

Create turtles

The command **crt** *number* creates the number of turtles specified by *number*. Turtles are created in the center of the screen. Experiment with creating one or more turtles to discover their colors and headings.

Move turtles

The command **fd** *step* moves each turtle forward the number of steps specified by *step*. Try: **fd 4**. Watch what happens when a turtle walks off the edge of the screen. The command **bk** *step* moves each turtle back the specified number of steps (but doesn't turn the turtle around).

Change turtle direction

Turtle direction can be changed in several ways. One way is to rotate all of the turtles some number of degrees using the command **rt** *angle* where *angle* is the number of degrees you want the turtles to rotate clockwise. Try: **rt 45**. You can use **lt** *angle* in the same way. You can also set all turtles to the same heading using the command **seth** *direction* where *direction* is the heading on a compass (0 is towards the top of the screen) that you want the turtles facing. Try: **seth 45**.

Change turtle color

Turtle color can be changed with the **setc** *newcolor* command, which changes all of the turtles to the color specified by *newcolor*. Note that *newcolor* can be simple color names (e.g., **red** or **blue**) or any number from 0 to 139. Try: **setc 105** or **setc blue**.

Have turtles draw paths

Each turtle has a pen that can be in the up or down position. You can control this using the **pu** (**p**en **u**p) and **pd** (**p**en **d**own) commands. If a turtle's pen is down, it leaves a trail wherever it goes.

Repeat a given statement multiple times

The statement **repeat** *times* **[***statements***]** will repeat the *statements* inside the square brackets the number of *times* you specify. For example, if you wanted a turtle to move forward 10 steps and turn right 30 degrees 5 times in a row you would use the statement **repeat 5 [fd 10 rt 30]**.

depending on which one is able to execute *statements*

Clear all of the turtles and patches

The command **ca** removes all of the turtles and resets the patches to black.

Remove all turtles from the world

The command **ct** kills all turtles but leaves the patches alone.

Turn all of the patches black

The command **cg** clears the **Graphics Canvas**, by resetting all of the patches to black, but does not kill the turtles.

Creating Sliders

As you experiment with some of the buttons, you may notice that you are trying to find just the right value for the number of steps you want the turtles to walk forward or the number of degrees you want them to turn. Instead of retyping the values each time, you can use sliders to change these values. There are three steps to using a slider: Creating a new slider, naming the slider, and then using the slider name instead of a number inside the button. This process is most easily illustrated in an example. The following steps create a slider that specifies the color of all of the turtles and a button that changes their color:

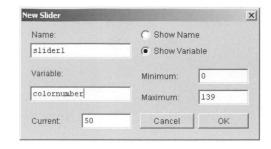

A slider editor.

❶ Create a new slider by going to the **Toolbar** and clicking on the green slider icon.

❷ Click and drag in the **Interface** area where you want the slider to go.

❸ A slider editor for the new slider will pop up ❺. Type the name **colornumber** in the space called **Variable**, and enter 0 as the minimum value, 139 as the maximum value, and 50 as the current value.

❹ Click **OK**.

Paint Tools

You can create turtles and color patches using the **Paint Tools.** To enter the painting mode and get to the **Paint Tools**, click on the paintbrush icon in the **Main Toolbar**. Once you are in painting mode, you can paint the patches by choosing the color you want from the Color palette (the color will appear in the square above the turtle in the picture) and then clicking on a paint tool like the pencil or the paint bucket ❻. As you paint with these tools on the **Graphics Canvas**, you will be coloring the underlying patches.

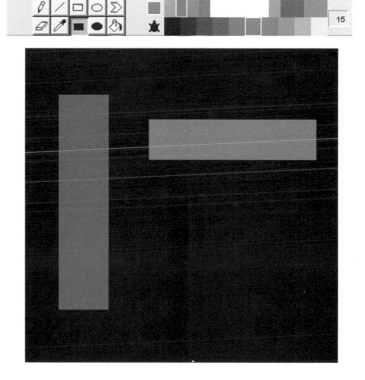

The Paint and Color Toolbars and the Graphics Canvas.

If, instead of patches, you would like to add new turtles to your StarLogo project, click on the turtle just under the colored square. Now when you choose a painting tool like the pencil or the paint bucket, you will be painting new turtles into your project! If you type **fd 1** in the **Turtle Command Center**, all of those new turtles will move. You can exit paint mode by clicking on the arrow tool. If you want to move a turtle by hand, then click on it and drag it around by holding the mouse button down (make sure that you have the arrow selected, not the paintbrush). Remember, however, that you won't be able to drag the patches because they are not mobile.

Landmark Decisions

Can you make your turtles react to obstacles in their environment? Perhaps you can make your turtles walk along a path that you create, such as the one shown below, by drawing obstacles that guide the turtles.

You can paint colors in the turtles' environment and then use the following procedure to make the turtles react to the colors as they move:

```
to check-patches
  if pc-ahead = red [rt 180]
  if pc-ahead = green [lt 90]
  if pc-ahead = blue [rt 90]
end
```

Try building a StarLogo project that has turtles walking on a particular path or reacting to obstacles in the environment in a meaningful way. Be sure to put the **check-patches** procedure in the **Turtle Procedures Pane 7 8**. If you want to see an example that uses these commands, check out the *Bumper Turtles* project in the Adventures Projects folder.

EXPLORATIONS

POSSIBLE

◆ As you are drawing obstacles on the screen, consider whether you want the obstacles to take up a lot or a little of the screen.

◆ Try making slight alterations to the location of your obstacles. How do these modifications affect the paths that the turtles follow?

◆ Experiment with different path widths and vary the number of turtles simultaneously walking on the path. When you create multiple turtles, do all of them walk the same way?

◆ Try adding a small amount of randomness to each step as the turtles walk.

◆ Think about real-world metaphors for the **check-patches** procedure. What do they suggest about how you might program the turtles or build the obstacles?

Command Centers

Start by typing some commands in the two **Command Centers**. Play around with moving your turtles, changing their colors, clearing the screen, and creating additional turtles. The **Command Centers** are good places to test new commands. To run commands, just type them and press **Return**. You can put many commands in a **Command Center**. If you put more than one command on a single line, then all of the commands on that line will be run when you press **Return**. When you are comfortable running both Turtle and Observer Commands, then you can begin writing procedures.

Procedures

In this Challenge, you will encounter procedures, possibly for the first time. Procedures are just combinations of commands that tell StarLogo how to execute compound actions. You can think about new procedures as ways to teach StarLogo new words. Every time you write a new procedure, you are "teaching" StarLogo a new word. You convey this to StarLogo by starting procedures with the word **to** and finishing with the word **end** as in the Turtle Procedure **to dance** (see chart at right).

to dance	In English this reads:
fd 10	move forward ten steps
wait 1	wait one second
bk 2	move back two steps
wait 1	wait one second
rt 75	turn right 75 degrees
fd 3	move forward three steps
end	

Everything between **to dance** and **end** tells StarLogo what you mean when you call the procedure **dance**. Notice that this procedure is designed for turtles, which means that you should write it in the **Turtle Procedures Pane**. Notice also that this procedure assumes that you already have turtles 🍎. If you don't have any, then use the **crt** command in the **Observer Command Center** to create some. Now try typing the **dance** procedure in the **Turtle Procedures Pane** and then typing **dance** in the **Turtle Command Center**. What happens if you make a **Forever** button with **dance** as the instruction?

The core of this Challenge is a short procedure that the turtles use to turn in different directions depending on the color of the patch that they "see" in front of them. This procedure is a Turtle Procedure because it is the turtles who are individually checking the patches directly in front of them.

to check-patches	In English this reads:
if pc-ahead = red [rt 180]	if the patch color one step ahead of me is red, then turn around
if pc-ahead = green [lt 90]	if the patch color one step ahead of me is green, then turn left
if pc-ahead = blue [rt 90]	if the patch color one step ahead of me is blue, then turn right
end	

Once you have written this procedure, you can just type **check-patches** in the **Turtle Command Center**. The turtles will understand what you mean and will execute those three commands.

Bumper Turtles

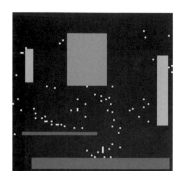

The Bumper Turtles' Graphics Canvas.

In this project, the turtles change direction every time they bounce off of an "obstacle." Depending on the color of the obstacle, the turtle will turn either to the right, to the left, or all the way around.

Click the **setup** button to set up the turtle in its initial position. Then click the **go** button to start the simulation. If you want to try adding some randomness to the turtle's path, stop the **go** button and then press the **go and wiggle** button.

By using the **pen-down** and **pen-up** buttons, you can control whether or not the turtle marks the path that it follows by drawing on the patches with its pen. To erase the turtle's path use **clear-path**, which clears only the yellow path drawn by the turtle.

The Interface from Bumper Turtles.

Follow the Leader

This project starts off like *Bumper Turtles* with a turtle checking patch color and turning accordingly. The first turtle in this project, however, draws with its pen down, leaving a path behind it. When a second turtle is created, it begins in a slightly different location than the first turtle. Notice that when this turtle starts moving it winds up following the path of the first turtle. This demonstrates a simple way that the first turtle can influence the environment and subsequently affect the behavior of another turtle. You will explore this idea more extensively in the Challenge 4.

The Interface from Follow the Leader.

To use this project, click on the **setup first turtle** button. Then click the **go** button to see the first turtle draw its path. Now, click **setup second turtle** and then **go** and watch what happens. Try clicking the **setup second turtle** button and pressing **go** several times. What happens if you press the **clear** button and then setup the second turtle?

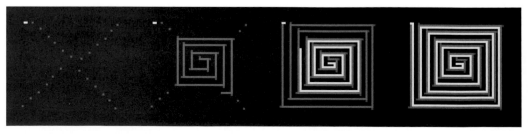

Follow the Leader's Graphics Canvas over time.

Yellow Brick Road

This project introduces a real-world metaphor for the **check-patches** procedure. The creators of this project changed **check-patches** to **check-color**. As the turtles (or "cars" in this model) **check-color**, they adjust their speeds according to the color of the patch ahead of them. The car speeds are controlled using the sliders **car1_speed** and **car2_speed**. Notice that only one car pays attention to the **Red_Zone**.

By adjusting the sliders, you can manipulate the speed of the cars on the track. What would this project look like if there were many more cars? How could you change the project to include intersections? Can you think of a way to let the cars choose whether to turn right or left? The following commands may be useful as you proceed 🍎.

If you want to...	Use these commands:	For this character:
Find out the patch color of the patch that a turtle is sitting on	The command **pc** returns the color of the patch that a turtle is on.	
Get the color of the patch directly in front of a turtle	The command **pc-ahead** returns the color of the patch directly in front of a turtle 🍎.	
Find out the patch color of a specific patch	The command **pc-at** *x-coordinate y-coordinate* returns the patch color of that individual patch, relative to the character's position (the observer always "sits" at 0 0 while the turtles can be anywhere). Try typing **show pc-at 1 1** in both the **Turtle** and **Observer Command Centers** and see what happens.	
Generate a random number	The command **random** *number* will generate a random number from 0 to *number* – 1. For example, **random 3** will return 0, 1, or 2.	
Do something only if a certain condition is satisfied	The conditional **if** *condition* **[***statement***]** will execute *statement* if the stated *condition* is true. For example, the statement **if (pc = red) [rt 90]** will cause all turtles on red patches to turn 90 degrees to the right.	depending on whether Turtle or Observer Commands make up the *statement*

Turning Turtles Into Termites

There are many types of interactions that can occur between creatures and their environment. In this Challenge, you can choose to model one of two different types of interactions. You can create a project in which turtles alter their behavior based on environmental characteristics, or you can design and build a project in which turtles change their environment.

If you choose the first option, then create a project in which the environment influences the turtles in more than one way. Start by thinking about new ways that the environment can change turtle behavior. You might build a world of patches that affect the turtles' position, color, or speed in different ways. Your project should be more ambitious than the one you completed for Challenge 3. To see an example of this kind of project, check out *Speeding Bumper Turtles*.

If you choose the second option, then build a project that asks the turtles to manipulate the patches in their environment. Perhaps your turtles will "move" objects (represented by patches) as in the *Turtledozers* or *Termites* projects. Alternatively, your turtles could change the patch colors as they walk across the **Graphics Canvas**. You can explore how these modifications to the environment change the turtles' behavior.

EXPLORATIONS

POSSIBLE

◆ Try programming the turtles to draw paths in colors that also influence their movement.

◆ Experiment with combining turtle and patch activity. Perhaps patches of a certain color influence turtles and turtles change the color of each patch they walk across.

◆ What happens in your project if the patches change color randomly?

◆ See what happens if turtles multiply when they run into certain patches. Are the effects of **hatch** and **sprout** identical?

◆ Explore the results if patches affect absolute headings instead of relative headings.

◆ Think about some real-world systems in which living things interact with their environment. Try to incorporate some of those ideas in your project.

Speeding Bumper Turtles

This project introduces the simple use of sliders to control how the turtles react to obstacles in their environment. In any model, sliders control values that anyone can easily change. Often, even a small change in a slider will cause a noticeable change in how the whole system looks or behaves.

Speeding Bumper Turtles is similar to the **Bumper Turtles** project in the previous Challenge, except that in this project the turtles' speeds change every time they bounce off of a colored obstacle. The speed associated with each obstacle is determined by the corresponding slider value. Take a look at the procedures to see how this behavior is implemented. Remember, every time you see **red-speed**, **green-speed**, or **blue-speed** in the procedures code, the program is reading the current value from the corresponding slider.

Click the **setup** button to set up the turtles at their initial positions. Click the **go** button to start the simulation. At any time, you can change the value of each of the speed sliders, **green-speed**, **red-speed**, and **blue-speed**. The value of each slider determines the speed that the turtles assume after they bounce off of a colored patch. You can also set the **number** slider to determine the number of turtles in the project. This change takes effect only when you **setup** the simulation again. If you want to draw a new set of obstacles, press **clear-graphics** and draw new obstacles using the **Paint Tools**. According to the existing procedures, the obstacles need to be blue, red, or green for the turtles to react to them, but you can make the obstacles in any shape or location that you wish.

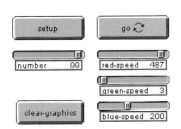
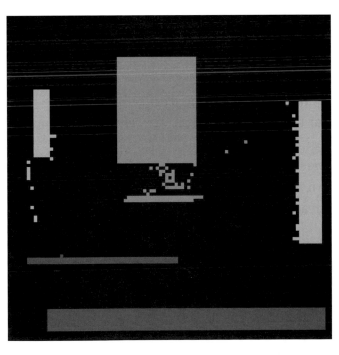

The Speeding Bumper Turtles project.

CHALLENGE HINTS

Create a new variable energy for all turtles	The statement **turtles-own [energy]** creates a new variable **energy** and allows you to use the set of commands that manipulate the turtles' **energy**.	This statement should be placed at the top of the **Turtle Procedures Pane**.
Set the value of energy for all turtles	The command **setenergy** *value* sets the variable **energy** to the *value* specified. Note that **setenergy** is one word.	
Increase the value of energy for all turtles	The command **setenergy energy +** *increase* adds the amount *increase* to the current energy level. Note that this is really the same as the last entry (**setenergy** *value*) with the *value* equal to the current **energy** plus an *increase*. Also, note the spaces on both sides of the plus sign.	
Do something to a turtle if its energy is above some value	Use the command **if energy >** *check* **[***statements***]** to cause turtles with an **energy** value greater than *check* to perform the *statements*.	

Multiply the energy of turtles who satisfy a certain condition	Use the statement
	   if *condition*
	    [setenergy energy * *multiplier***]**
	to ask those turtles who satisfy the *condition* to multiply their **energy** by the *multiplier*.
	Try: **if color = blue [setenergy energy * 1.5]**.	

Energizer Turtles

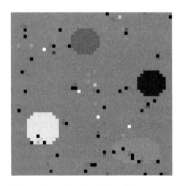

Energizer Turtles' Graphics Canvas.

A straightforward example of using a variable is shown in the project *Energizer Turtles*. This project builds on the *Bumper Turtles* series of projects. In this case when the turtles walk over patches of different colors their **energy** either increases or decreases, depending on the color of the patch that they pass. The turtles gain **energy** if they step on a red or yellow patch. They lose **energy** if they step on a blue or gray patch. The energy level of each turtle is indicated by its color (a more energetic turtle is brighter) as well as by how fast it moves (a more energetic turtle moves faster).

As you explore this project, there are a couple of details to notice in the procedures. First, a modified **check-patches** procedure asks each turtle to increase or decrease its **energy** depending on the patch color at its location. Second, a turtle's **energy** affects both its color and its speed. The **fd** command uses the value of the turtle's **energy** variable to determine the size of the turtle's forward step each time it moves. The **scale-color** command sets the turtles with the most **energy** to almost white and the least **energy** to almost black, with the turtles in between showing varying shades of **blue**. The **scale-color** command takes four arguments (or inputs), so it is worth a quick look. This program uses the following command:

scale-color blue energy 0 20

This command literally means, scale the color of the turtles to a shade of **blue**, depending on the value of the **energy** variable, with an **energy** value of **0** resulting in very dark blue and **20** in very light blue.

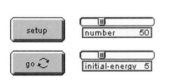

Energizer Turtles' Interface.

To try this project, click the **setup** button to create the number of turtles shown on the **number** slider. You can add "energy-change patches" by drawing red, yellow, blue, or gray patches. Click the **go** button to start the simulation and see the effect of the colored patches on the color and the speed of the turtles. You may notice that turtles tend to get stuck in some of the patches that decrease their **energy**. Can you modify the percentage increase or decrease in the turtles' **energy** (in the Turtle Procedures) to change this tendency?

Rabbits

Another project that uses the energy concept is *Rabbits*. This project explores a simple ecosystem made up of rabbits and grass. The rabbits wander around randomly, and the grass grows randomly. Rabbits use up **energy** as they move. When a rabbit bumps into some grass, it eats the grass and gains **energy**. If the rabbit gains enough **energy**, then it "reproduces" by hatching a new rabbit. If it loses all of its **energy**, then the rabbit dies.

Click the **setup** button to set up the rabbits (red) and grass (green). The **number** slider controls the initial number of rabbits. Click the **go** button to start the simulation. The **hatch-threshold** slider sets the energy level at which the rabbits reproduce. The **grass-rate** slider controls the rate at which the grass grows. (Note: You cannot change the **grass-rate** in the middle of a simulation. The change takes effect at the next **setup**.)

Rabbits' Interface.

Teaching Turtles to Talk

They say that misery loves company and that there is safety in numbers. The turtles in this Challenge have their own clichés—"turtles love company" and "there is happiness in numbers." The turtles adopted these expressions because their **happiness** increases when they share a patch with another turtle.

To begin this Challenge you can explore the projects *Shiny Happy Turtles 1* and *Shiny Happy Turtles 2*, which demonstrate two different ways that a turtle can gain **happiness** when it shares a patch with another turtle. See if you can figure out how the turtles increase their **happiness** in these projects. What methods are used in each project to affect the turtle behavior? What patterns of behavior can you identify in each project?

Next, look at the heart of these two projects (the procedures **friends-meet** and **set-avghappy**) and create your own project that enables turtles to affect the **happiness** of other turtles. You can try experimenting with *methods for* increasing and decreasing **happiness** or exploring the *effects of* increased or decreased **happiness**. Your Challenge is to create a project, incorporating principles from the sample projects, that enables turtles to influence each other's **happiness** and react to their own levels of **happiness**.

EXPLORATIONS

POSSIBLE

◆ Think of a situation in which turtles might be unhappy if there were other turtles nearby. Try to implement this in your project.

◆ Look at what happens if **happiness** causes turtles to slow down or move in a different pattern. What happens if happy turtles alter their environment?

◆ Can you think of any animals that are happy when they stick close together? Are there any costs or benefits from that behavior? How would you model that kind of system?

◆ Some organisms behave differently when they are crowded. Can you think of an example of this kind of behavior? Can you create a model to illustrate your example?

Shiny Happy Turtles 1

This project builds on the principles introduced in the *Energizer Turtles* project from Challenge 5. The turtles in this project are born with a state of **happiness** (a turtle variable similar to **energy** in Challenge 5). Turtles' **happiness** can increase or decrease as they interact with their environment and with other turtles.

The Graphics Canvas from Shiny Happy Turtles 1.

Two turtle-environment interactions are modeled in this project. When turtles are in the red "cinema" patches, they gain or lose **happiness** based on the settings in the **cinema** slider. Similarly, turtles gain or lose **happiness** in the blue "school" patches based on the value of the **school** slider.

Turtle-turtle interaction is also modeled in this project. When the turtles find themselves alone on a patch, they lose a small amount of **happiness**. But when turtles find themselves sharing a patch with another turtle, they double their **happiness**. The assumption underlying this model is that turtles are happier when they are in contact with other turtles.

Turtles express their **happiness** in three ways. First, happier turtles move faster. Second, happier turtles are lighter in color (very light green as compared to dark green). Finally, happier turtles tend to circle to their right, aiming to get back to the place that made them happy, while unhappy turtles tend to keep moving in a straight line as they look for a more pleasant environment.

To start the simulation, click **setup** to create the number of turtles indicated on the **number** slider. Each turtle is created with a random level of **happiness**. You can adjust the maximum value using the **initial-happiness** slider. Click **go** to watch the turtles interact with each other and with their environment. You can change the influence exerted by the movies and the school by increasing or decreasing values of the **school** and **cinema** sliders. The slider values control the percentage of increase or decrease in **happiness** of a turtle when it occupies the school or cinema patches.

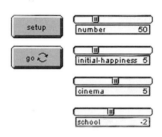

The Interface from Shiny Happy Turtles 1.

Shiny Happy Turtles 2

The interface and most of the principles of *Shiny Happy Turtles 2* are exactly the same as those in *Shiny Happy Turtles 1*. Play with *Shiny Happy Turtles 2* for a little while. Can you tell what is different about this project based on your observations of the turtle-turtle and turtle-environment interactions? What unique patterns can you identify in this project?

In *Shiny Happy Turtles 2*, when two turtles share a patch they average their two **happiness** values (and add 10 percent for good fortune). These turtle-turtle interactions can lead to noticeably different patterns than the kind you observed in *Shiny Happy Turtles 1*. Watch what happens when a really happy turtle meets a really unhappy turtle. A good place to look for this is in a patch that causes turtles to lose **happiness**. What other kinds of interactions can you see in *Shiny Happy Turtles 2*?

Turtle-Turtle Commands

You will need the following commands to implement basic turtle-turtle interactions in your own projects.

If you want to...   **Use these commands:**   **For this character:**

CHALLENGE HINTS

Do one thing if a certain condition is satisfied, and do something else if that condition is not satisfied

The conditional
ifelse *condition*
   [*statement1***] [***statement2***]**
executes *statement1* if the stated condition is true and *statement2* if it is false. For example, the statement
ifelse color = blue
   [rt 90] [lt 90]
causes all blue turtles to turn right 90 degrees and all other turtles to turn left 90 degrees.

depending on whether Turtle or Observer Commands make up *statement1* and *statement2*

Find out if there are any other turtles on a patch

The command **count-turtles-here** returns the number of turtles on a patch.

Get the who number of another turtle that is on your patch

The command **one-of-turtles-here** returns the **who** number of another turtle on a patch, if there is another turtle present. If there are no other turtles present, then −1 is returned.

Get the value of a variable from another turtle

Use the command
set*variable1* **(***variable2***-of one-of-turtles-here)**
to get a variable value from another turtle. *variable1* is the name of the variable you are using to store the value of *variable2* from the other turtle. For example:
setotherage (age-of one-of-turtles-here) stores the second turtle's **age** in the first turtle's variable **otherage**.

This code segment requires the following declaration of two turtle variables at the top of the **Turtle Procedures Pane**:
turtles-own [age otherage]

One note about turtles on patches: An individual turtle is always sitting on a patch, so there will always be *one* turtle on a patch (itself!) when you ask a turtle to look and see how many turtles occupy its patch (by using **count-turtles-here**). Therefore, if you are interested in identifying turtles who are sharing a patch with at least one other turtle, you will need to make sure that **count-turtles-here** is greater than one.

CHALLENGE 7

Quest for Communication

In the project **Castle Invasion**, turtles try to gain entrance to a castle, but the entrance is protected with a code. In order to gain access, a turtle needs to know four code words. A turtle can learn these words by running over four colored patches that hold the secret words. Watch the turtles learn the code words. How long does it take them to get into the castle? What happens if more patches hold the secret words?

The turtles need to figure out a faster way to get back into the castle. Your Challenge is to help them work together so that they can enter the castle more quickly. By sharing the code words that they already know, the turtles can help each other get into the castle.

Using the command **grab**, you can instruct the turtles to exchange code words with one another. Try to determine if the enhanced information exchange affects how quickly the turtles can break into the castle. What happens if you modify the way that they exchange information? How does this change affect the time it takes them to gain access to the castle? The **Collisions** project illustrates a different use of **grab**.

The turtle-turtle communication algorithms used to model this information transfer are powerful components of any modeling environment. Modeling interactions among creatures can enrich your existing models and broaden the scope of models you can create.

EXPLORATIONS

◆ What happens if the turtles do not go directly to the castle once they know all four words? What else might you do with these turtles? How does this model compare to team projects in which no one person gets credit until the entire team has completed the project?

◆ Try making a model where turtles exchange information based on a certain probability.

◆ How do you think information exchange and eventual castle entry will be affected if the turtles occasionally forget words? Can you implement that modification?

◆ What if there were a cost (losing all of the known code words, dying, etc.) when a turtle tried to enter the castle without knowing all of the words?

◆ What happens to the length of time to castle entry if you change the number of turtles? What if you change the number of code words?

◆ Apply this type of turtle-turtle communication to other projects that you have been working on.

Teaching turtles to communicate with each other is a three-step process. First, turtle one (let's call him Michelangelo) must identify the turtle to whom he is talking. One way to do this is to ask Michelangelo to **grab** a **partner**. If Michelangelo sees another turtle on his patch, he grabs the turtle and sets his turtle variable **partner** to the **who** number of the second turtle (let's call him Donatello). Once the turtle variable **partner** is set, Michelangelo can converse with Donatello until he releases Donatello as his **partner**.

You don't need to create the turtle variable **partner**. All turtles are born with the capability to store identification information for partners. Try creating 100 moving red turtles who continually run the following procedure as they move 🍎 :

```
to talk
    grab one-of-turtles-here
        [setc-of partner blue]
end
```

Castle Invasion

To see the effects of this kind of turtle-turtle communication you will explore and modify the **Castle Invasion** project. In this project there is a four-word code that the turtles must learn before they can enter the castle. Initially, the turtles do not know any of the four code words. Scattered across the **Graphics Canvas** are four color-coded patches, each hiding one of the four code words. When the turtles visit one of these patches, they learn the code word associated with that patch. As the turtles learn more words, they turn darker shades of purple. When they successfully learn all four words they turn a very dark shade of purple and are transported inside the castle. The monitors keep track of the total time that has passed and the number of turtles who have gained access to the castle.

To start the simulation, click **setup** to create the castle, the special "code" patches, and the turtles on the screen. All turtles start in the center of the screen. When you click on the **go** button, the turtles will move and gather code words. You can keep track of the total time it takes for the first turtle to gain access to the castle by watching the **time** monitor. You will know when turtles arrive at the castle by looking for them at the castle door and by checking the **count-turtles** monitor, which keeps track of the number of turtles inside the castle.

Castle Invasion's Graphics Canvas and Interface.

You can track the progress of individual turtles by opening their turtle monitors and examining which words they know (stored in the turtle variables **code1** to **code4**). The four code words are variables that take words, instead of numbers, as values. To define a variable in this way, list the set of acceptable words in square brackets immediately following the variable name:

turtles-own [code1 [none oh] code2 [none this]]

Now, **code1** can take the value **none** or **oh**. Once you have defined a variable in this manner, you should use the acceptable words in place of numeric values for the variable. For example, you can set **code2** to **this** using:

setcode2 this

Modifying *Castle Invasion* is the heart of this Challenge. You are responsible for giving the turtles a new way to gather information about the code words. By adding turtle-turtle communication to the turtles' means of collecting information, turtles will be able to exchange code words with each other. Adding the following commands will allow a turtle to get the first code word from another turtle who already knows it 🕖.

```grab one-of-turtles-here [if (code1 = none) and ((code1-of other) not= none) [setcode1 code1-of partner setnumber number + 1]] ```	**In English this reads:** If there is another turtle here, grab that turtle and set your variable partner to that turtle's who number. If you don't know code1 and if the other turtle does know code1, then learn code1 from your partner and increase the number of words you know by 1.

The grabbing turtle keeps the same **partner** until the end of the instruction list (the last square bracket ends the **grab** by releasing the turtle's **partner**).

You can add similar commands to enable the turtles to exchange the other three code words. Then, when turtles bump into one another, they will share all of the information that they have gathered.

The **grab** command is key to implementing turtle-turtle communication in your projects. Spend some time becoming comfortable with the Turtle Commands on the next page that are used to exchange information.

CHALLENGE HINTS

If you want to...	Use these commands:	For this character:
Talk to another turtle	The command **grab *selectedturtle* [*statements*]** allows a turtle to select a **partner** and then run the ***statements***. ***selectedturtle*** is any command that returns a turtle's **who** number. A turtle only keeps his **partner** for the duration of the ***statements***.	
Look at the variable of another turtle	The command ***variable1*-of *whonumber*** allows a turtle to inspect another turtle's ***variable1***. ***whonumber*** can be a number or a command that returns a **who** such as **partner** or **one-of-turtles-here**. For example: **if ((color-of partner) = blue) [setc red]** allows a turtle to check to see if his **partner** is blue and, if so, change his own **color** to red. The parentheses are required in this command.	
Change another turtle's variable	The command ***setvariable2*-of *whonumber newvalue*** changes the other turtle's ***variable2*** to the ***newvalue*** you specify. For example, **setc-of 3 blue** changes the **color** of turtle three to blue.	
Execute commands if something is not true	Use a traditional **if** statement with the command **not=** to carry out instructions if a condition is not met. **if (color not= red) [*statement*]** runs the ***statement*** only if the turtle **color** is not red 🍎.	
Define a variable that takes word values instead of numeric values	The statement **turtles-own [*variablename* [*word1 word2*]]** creates a new variable ***variablename***, and allows you to set its value to ***word1*** or ***word2***. For instance, you can create a variable **transport** that can take on four possible values: **turtles-own [transport [car boat truck train]]**	

Collisions

This project is an idea model of a particle system that illustrates the use of **grab**. In ***Collisions***, particles bounce off of walls and off of each other. They conserve energy, but not momentum, when they collide. Once a turtle has grabbed a **partner** in the **collide** procedure, it runs all of the instructions in between the square brackets. If a turtle doesn't find a **partner** to **grab**, then it skips all of those instructions and continues going.

Set the **number** slider to the desired number of particles, then press **setup** and **go**. Can you see any collisions? Is it any easier to track the collisions when the turtles' pens are down? When the turtles take large steps they sometimes jump over one another. Can you reduce their forward step size to eliminate this effect?

The Collisions' Interface.

The Plot Thickens

Often, interesting patterns emerge from the rules that the turtles follow in your StarLogo projects. Observing the evolution of these patterns can be captivating. But direct observation rarely provides reliable quantitative information about the whole turtle population. Your Challenge is to design and implement an innovative method to display turtle information. You might begin by creating a line graph, using the StarLogo **Plot Window** to visualize the changes in your model over time, or by using global monitors to keep track of aggregate information about your turtles. After exploring these built-in features, create your own graphic illustration using the turtles themselves to display information in a meaningful way.

In this Challenge, you can build your illustration in one of your own projects or a sample project. You can use the commands **setx** *position* and **sety** *position* to arrange the turtles.

Once you have created your graph, verify that the turtles are displaying information in the manner that you intended. One way to determine the accuracy of your illustration is to open up the **Turtle Monitors**. Can you figure out if all of the turtles are in the right place? What information is most clearly displayed in your graph? What information is missing? The projects *Disease* and *Reaction* show some new types of illustrations and allow you to restart the simulation after viewing an illustration by pressing the **go-back** and **go** buttons.

EXPLORATIONS

◆ Which type of graphic illustration allows you to make better predictions about the system?

◆ How do your graphs differ from StarLogo's built-in tools (global monitors and time series plots)? When are you likely to use the plotting tool? Your own graph? When is a global monitor useful?

◆ Can you think of other ways to implement turtle-based graphs? Perhaps you could ask the turtles to gather in circles that show their state. Or you could ask the turtles to line up using a different variable.

◆ Try modifying one aspect of the project that you are using. Can you see the effects of this change in your graph?

Disease

In this sample project, a disease afflicts the turtle population. Though most turtles start out healthy, many eventually succumb to the disease. When a turtle is infected, by sharing a patch with an infected turtle, it becomes a latent carrier of the disease. Soon it becomes sick and displays symptoms of the disease. Eventually, it recovers or dies. Recovered turtles are no longer susceptible to the disease.

Turtles contract the disease from other infected turtles with the probability specified by the **infect-rate** slider and recover with the probability specified by the **recover-rate** slider. Turtles remain latent for **latent-time** and sick for **sick-time**. You can specify the initial conditions of the simulation with the **number** and **infected** sliders.

Press **stop-it** and use the **pop-dist** button to create a distribution of turtles by **age**, with the youngest turtles on the left. The height of each line shows how many turtles fall into a particular age bracket. Open a few **Turtle Monitors** to see if all of the turtles are in the correct position. You can restart the simulation by pressing **start** or by first asking the turtles to **go-back** to their previous positions and then pressing **start**.

The Disease project and bar graph.

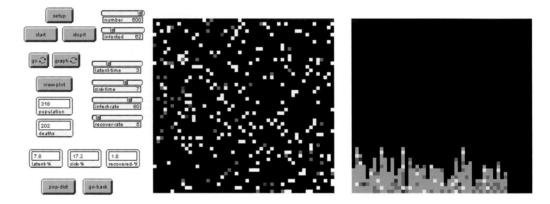

Reaction

Reaction employs five different turtle colors to simulate the following system of reversible chemical reactions:

	In English this reads:
Reaction 1: red + blue ↔ yellow	Reaction 1: When a red turtle encounters a blue turtle, they combine to form a yellow turtle. Sometimes a yellow turtle decomposes into a red turtle and a blue turtle.
Reaction 2: yellow + white ↔ green	Reaction 2: When a yellow turtle encounters a white turtle, they combine to form a green turtle. Sometimes a green turtle decomposes into a yellow turtle and a white turtle.

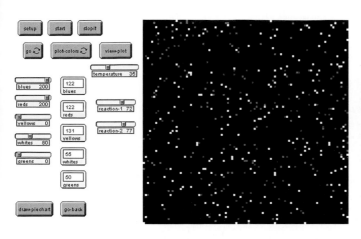

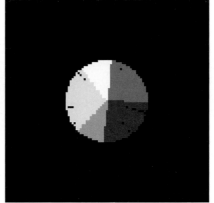

The Reaction project and a pie chart.

You can control the probability of the forward reactions using the **reaction-1** and **reaction-2** sliders. The probability of the reverse reactions is defined as 1 minus the probability of the forward reactions. Adjusting the **temperature** slider controls the speed of molecular movement. To change the initial conditions, simply reset the color sliders.

Stop the simulation, and then click on the **draw-piechart** button to display the relative concentrations of the molecules. You can start the simulation again by pressing **start** or **go-back** and then **start**.

Global Monitors

Both sample projects use global monitors to display precise numerical data about the population of turtles. Look at the code for the **sick-%** monitor in *Disease* by **Control** double-clicking (or **Shift** double-clicking on a Mac) on the monitor. It calls the Observer Procedure **sick-%**, which reads as follows:

```
to sick-%
    output ((count-turtles-with [health = sick]) * 100) / count-turtles
end
```

This procedure uses the command **output** to return a value.

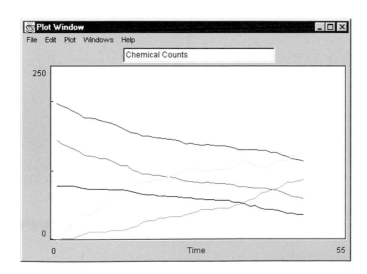

Plot Window from Reaction.

Building Time Series Plots

You can create time series plots in any project using the Observer Commands on the following page.

If you want to...	Use these commands:	For this character:
Select which number pen you want to issue a command to	The command **ppnumber** (where **number** is the number of the pen that you are selecting) tells StarLogo the pen to which you are going to issue a command. This command is followed by another command, such as **plot** or **ppreset**.	
Clear the whole plot	The command **clear-plot** resets the plot window.	
Clear the plot made by one of the pens	The command **ppreset** clears the plot made by whichever pen is currently selected.	
Choose the color of a plotting pen	The command **setppc** *color* sets the color of whichever pen is currently selected to the *color* that is specified.	
Set the plotting range on the x or y axes	The commands **setplot-xrange** *minimum maximum* and **setplot-yrange** *minimum maximum* set the x- and y-plot ranges to the *minimum* and *maximum* values specified.	
Plot the current value of a variable as the y value and the current time step as the x value	The command **plot** *value* directs the selected pen to **plot** a point on the graph on the y-axis at the *value* specified and on the x-axis at the next available value. By default the points are connected by a line.	
Plot individual points	The command **ppu** (for **p**lot **p**en **u**p) causes the plot pen to draw x's instead of plotting a continuous line. Use **ppd** to switch back to a continuous line.	
Put a title on your plot	The command **setplot-title** *"name"* sets the plot title to *name* ⬚.	
Label the plot axes	The commands **setplot-xlabel** *"x-axis name"* and **setplot-ylabel** *"y-axis name"* allow you to put labels on the axes of your plot.	

CHALLENGE HINTS

CHALLENGE 9

How to Track a Turtle

Do you feel as if you have been wandering around aimlessly? Have you been traveling across patches with no particular destination? Do you wish that you could gain some direction? Well, look no further! You can get the direction you desire from a command that lets you head towards any other turtle, as long as you know its **who** number. That versatile command is:

seth towards
   xcor-of *whonumber*
   ycor-of *whonumber*

This command sets the **heading** of the turtles in the direction of the turtle *whonumber*.

Now that you know the secret to finding some direction, build a project in which turtles head towards a moving target (another turtle). You might want to build this behavior into one of your previous projects or try starting with one of these ideas:

- Build a game of Tag in which the "it" chooses and seeks out its next target

- Create a model of a pickpocket on a crowded city square.

- Build a model of a lion hunting a zebra.

EXPLORATIONS

◆ Notice that in the sample project *Gotya* it is difficult to count the number of "tagged" turtles. Modify the project so that the last tagged turtle chases the turtle who was tagged immediately before it.

◆ Try building a project in which a shy turtle heads *away from* the paparazzi.

◆ Create a turtle who grabs a **partner** and then heads towards it. When the turtle reaches its **partner**, instruct it to drop that **partner** and select a new one. Does your model remind you of any real-world systems?

The procedure for instructing a turtle to follow another turtle is based on several new concepts. The command **seth towards *x-coordinate y-coordinate*** provides the basic framework for making a turtle head in a particular direction, towards the point specified by ***x-coordinate*** and ***y-coordinate***. For example, the command **seth towards 0 0** would make a turtle head towards the center of the screen (which is at location 0, 0).

If you want a turtle to head towards another turtle, you need to find out the location of the other turtle: You can use **xcor-of *whonumber*** to get the x-coordinate of the turtle and **ycor-of *whonumber*** to get the y-coordinate. Putting these concepts together results in the command:

> **seth towards (xcor-of *whonumber*) (ycor-of *whonumber*)**

which sets the **heading** of a turtle **towards** the turtle with the specified ***whonumber***. One use of this command is demonstrated in the sample project ***Gotya***.

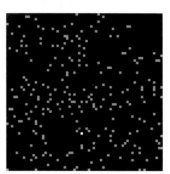

Gotya's Graphics Canvas over time.

Gotya

This project shows a clever way of using "heading towards." The turtles in ***Gotya*** play a version of Tag in which the first turtle (**who** number 0) is "it." The "it" turtle (white) and the pool of "taggable" turtles (green) run randomly around the screen. If the "it" turtle lands on an untagged turtle, "it" tags the other turtle by turning it red. When the appropriate switch is thrown, the tagged turtles follow the "it" turtle.

Gotya's Interface.

Click the **setup** button to create the number of turtles indicated on the **numturts** slider. One of those turtles is designated as "it" and colored white, while the others are untagged, green turtles. Instead of relying on numeric values to indicate a turtle's **caught** state in ***Gotya***, the words **yes**, **no**, and **it** are used instead.

When you click **go**, the turtles move randomly about the screen. It is captivating to watch the turtles move apart and back together as you toggle the **together** slider. Observing this process is a good way to get a feel for how turtles head towards other turtles. As you are reading through the code, be sure to look at the line **seth towards xcor-of 0 ycor-of 0**, which is the command that makes red turtles head towards the "it" turtle (whose **who** number is zero).

The interface for this project employs a true/false slider to regulate the tagged turtles' following behavior. As turtles get tagged, they follow "it" if the **together** slider is toggled to 1, and they move randomly if the slider is toggled to 0. The

count-tagged monitor keeps track of the total number of turtles who have been tagged, which is useful when the tagged turtles are bunched up behind "it." Finally, the **slow** button (which is scaled by the **time** slider) can be used to slow down the whole process if you'd like to watch the game more carefully.

Mouse Commands

You already know that turtles can follow other turtles, but you might not know that turtles can also follow mice—computer mice, that is. Turtles can locate the mouse on the **Graphics Canvas** and can even tell whether the mouse button is down. Using this information, the turtles can follow the mouse around the screen or run a command when you click the mouse button. Both the turtles and the observer can use the following mouse commands:

If you want to...	Use these commands:	For this character:
Find the coordinates of the current mouse location	The commands **mouse-xcor** and **mouse-ycor** return the x-coordinate and y-coordinate of the mouse as long as it is on the **Graphics Canvas**. For example the Turtle Command, **seth towards mouse-xcor mouse y-cor** points turtles **towards** the current mouse location.	
Find out whether the mouse button is pressed	The command **mouse-down?** returns true if the mouse button is down and false if it is not.	

Breeds—The Final Frontier

Until now you have been addressing all of the individuals in your projects as turtles. You can use **breeds** of turtles to give different groups of turtles their own unique behaviors. Your Challenge is to create a project in which different kinds of turtles interact with one another in ways that reflect their identities. Use the Turtle Commands **one-of-*breeds*-here** and **if breed = *breed1* [*statements*]** as well as the Observer Command **ask-*breed1* [*statements*]** to direct groups of turtles in your project.

For instance, you could build:

- A demonstration of how electrons and protons join to form neutrons.

- A model of a high school dance. (With whom will you dance? On what will you base your decisions?)

- A simulation that illustrates how people's political opinions can be influenced by others.

- A model of a lion killing a zebra. (Note: This is a bit more difficult than just chasing the zebra.) Can you build a more complex ecosystem now?

EXPLORATIONS

POSSIBLE

◆ Brainstorm a list of possible topics for new StarLogo projects.

◆ Now that you have completed all of the Challenges, you are in the top echelon of StarLogo scholars. Try to integrate many of the concepts that you have covered and apply them to a system that interests you. Think about what you might want to learn from creating a model of your system, and what kinds of questions might arise from that model. Let these ideas guide your creation of many more StarLogo models.

Creating Breeds

Creating new **breeds** is as easy as creating new turtle variables. In fact, you can think of **breeds** as a special kind of turtle variable. If you open a Turtle Monitor, you will see **breed** in addition to **color**, **heading**, and so forth. If you have not created a **breed** yet, you will see that **breed** is set to zero. To create **breeds**, type **breeds [*breed1 breed2*]** at the very top of the **Turtle Procedures Pane** 🐢. In this statement *breed1* and *breed2* are sample breed names. You should make sure that you put all of the **breeds** on a single line and only type the **breeds** command once in any project. For instance, if you wanted to create the **breeds lions** and **tigers** and **bears**, you would type:

breeds [lions tigers bears]

Notice that, like turtle variables, there are no commas between the **breeds** and that you must put the **breeds** in between one set of square brackets.

Once you have created **breeds**, you will probably want to create some turtles of each breed type. To create and use turtles of particular **breeds**, you will need to use some new commands.

If you want to...	Use these commands:	For this character:
Create a new breed for all turtles	The statement **breeds [*breedname*]** creates a new breed *breedname*, and allows you to use a special set of commands to address only *breedname*. Try: **breeds [lions]**.	This statement should be placed at the top of the **Turtle Procedures Pane**.
Create turtles of a particular breed	The command **create-*breed1 number*** creates the number of turtles of type *breed1* specified by **number**. For example, to create 12 turtles of type lions you would use the command **create-lions 12**.	
Change a turtle from one breed to another	Use the command **setbreed *breed2*** to change an existing turtle from its current breed to *breed2*.	
Ask all lions to do something	The command **if breed = lions [*statements*]** instructs all of the **lions** to perform the *statements*.	
	The command **ask-lions [*statements*]** instructs all of the **lions** to perform the *statements*.	
Count the number of turtles in a breed	The command **count-*breed1*** returns the number of *breed1* turtles alive at that moment and can be used with any breed that you have created.	

CHALLENGE HINTS

A Sample Use of Breeds

The Turtle Command **one-of-turtles-here** returns the **who** of one of the turtles on the patch. So the code **if color = orange [setprey one-of-turtles-here]** instructs the orange turtles to set their **prey** variable to the **who** of one of the turtles on their patch.

If, however, you want to instruct an "orange cat" turtle to interact with a "purple mouse" turtle, you need to ensure that the **one-of-turtles-here** command returns a **who** from a purple turtle. But, there is no command:

one-of-turtles-here-with [color = purple]

You can solve this dilemma using breeds. Start by creating two **breeds**, **cats** and **mice**, and a turtle variable for **prey** as follows:

breeds [cats mice]
turtles-own [prey]

You can now ask the cats to set their sights on a mouse like this:

if breed = cats [setprey one-of-mice-here]

By using the command **one-of-mice-here**, you know that the **cats** will only record the **who** of one of the **mice**. Once the cat has selected a particular mouse as **prey**, you will have to tell it what to do with the mouse.

The following sample projects use **breeds** to differentiate behavior among turtles.

Traffic

This project models cars and trucks driving on a highway and swans swimming in a nearby river. Use the buttons **setup**, **go**, and **stop-it** to control the simulation. **number** controls the initial number of cars on the road. (You will have to **setup** the simulation again for a change in this slider to take effect.) **lookahead** controls how many spaces ahead each car looks to see if there is open driving room, and **speedup** and **slowdown** control the rates for acceleration and deceleration.

In this project there are four breeds:

breeds [lefts rights swans police]

If you look through the code, you will see that the swimming turtles have **breed = swans** and the driving turtles in the top lane have **breed = lefts** (similarly, those in the bottom lane have **breed = rights**). This project uses breeds to give different behaviors to different groups of turtles.

This project introduces a new way to ask turtles to perform tasks based on their breed. Earlier, you saw code that addressed breeds using an **if** statement such as:

if breed = swans [swim-in-the-river]

This project uses a different way of addressing breeds:

ask-swans [swim-in-the-river]

Both of these lines of code mean "if you are a turtle and your breed is swans, go swim-in-the-river." The difference between the two statements is that the command **if breed = swans [swim-in-the-river]** can only be executed by the turtles, while the command **ask-swans [swim-in-the-river]** can only be executed by the observer 🍎.

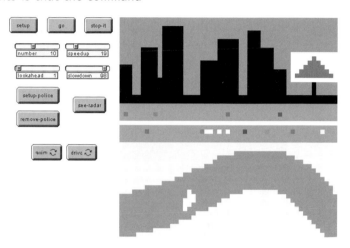

Similarly, **ask-lefts [drive-to-the-left]** (an Observer Command) ensures that only a subset of the cars on the screen will drive to the left. Notice that **ask-lefts** (just like **if breed = lefts**) requires that the set of instructions for the **lefts** be placed in between square brackets.

The cars in the traffic model follow three very simple rules:

❶ If there is a car ahead, then slow down.

❷ If there is no car ahead, then speed up.

❸ If you see a radar trap, then slow down.

The Traffic project.

Turtle Demographics

Turtle Demographics models the human population explosion. **setup** is used to establish initial populations, and **go** starts the simulation. The sliders, **Nevada-rate**, **Utah-rate**, and so forth, control the birth rates for the different states. You can watch the populations grow on the **Graphics Canvas**, and you can track the actual populations in the monitors and in the **Plot Window**.

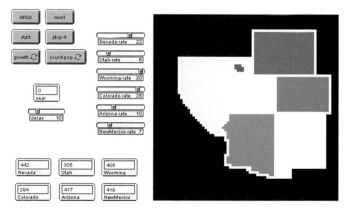

The Turtle Demographics project.

Breeds enable both the project and the user to distinguish between people in the various states. The different growth rates in the states mean that the turtles must know when to reproduce based on the growth rate for their state. Look at the **go** procedure. Notice that the turtles with **breed = nv** are following a different procedure than turtles with **breed = ut**. Turtles in each state reproduce when their breed is called upon to do so.

Notes for MacStarLogo Users

USING STARLOGO ON MACINTOSH COMPUTERS

There are several different versions of StarLogo that run on Macintosh computers. If you have a G3 or later (all iMacs and iBooks have at least G3 processors), we strongly recommend that you use the Java-based version of StarLogo (described in Chapter 6). If you are using an older Macintosh, you can use MacStarLogo, available on the CD included with this book or online at http://www.media.mit.edu/starlogo. There are two versions of MacStarLogo, one for PowerPC computers and one for 68K computers. Another option for Macintosh users is StarLogoT, which includes a slightly different set of features and is available at http://ccl.sesp.northwestern.edu/cm/starlogoT. The notes in this appendix are applicable for users of both MacStarLogo and StarLogoT.

MACSTARLOGO ADVENTURES PROJECTS

There is a separate set of Adventures Projects for MacStarLogo. These projects are functionally equivalent to the StarLogo projects, though some of the code looks a little bit different. When the code differs significantly, it will be detailed in the MacStarLogo notes at the end of this appendix. In addition, MacStarLogo comes with a slightly different set of Sample Projects for you to explore. You can find more information about these projects at http://www.media.mit.edu/macstarlogo/projects.

MACSTARLOGO USER INTERFACE

In MacStarLogo there are many separately labeled windows, which will be described below. In the Challenges, you will find many references to specific places within StarLogo, like the **Graphics Canvas** or the **Interface** area. In MacStarLogo each of these areas is a distinct window, like the **Graphics Window** or the **Interface Window**.

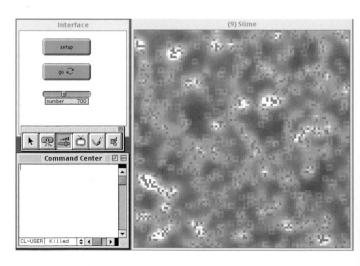

The Slime project in MacStarLogo.

Most MacStarLogo windows have similar names to their StarLogo counterparts. Below, we provide further information for those cases where MacStarLogo departs significantly from the Java implementation of StarLogo.

When you open a sample project in MacStarLogo, it will look something like the *Slime* project pictured at the bottom of the previous page. The main elements of the MacStarLogo interface are described below.

Graphics Window

The initially black **Graphics Window** is a grid of patches where the turtles live. This picture is from the *Slime* project, which is available in the Sample Projects folder. You can move a turtle directly by dragging it with the mouse. If you are fast, you can do this while the program is running.

You can change the size and shape of the **Graphics Window** and modify the size of the patches using the **Edit Settings...** menu. The **Graphics Window** "wraps," meaning that if a turtle walks off the right-hand side of the screen it will reappear on the left-hand side of the screen. The same is true of the top and bottom of the **Graphics Window**.

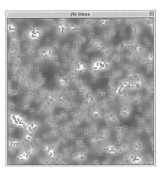

A MacStarLogo Graphics Window.

Interface Window

In the **Interface Window** you can create interface elements like buttons, sliders, and monitors that allow you to interact directly with your MacStarLogo projects. Pressing a button runs that button's commands. Adjusting a slider allows you to control the value of the variable, in this case **number**. This **Interface Window** (from the *Slime* project) has two buttons and one slider. The **go** button is currently running, as indicated by the darker color. You can add your own interface elements using the **Main Toolbar**. To learn more about buttons and sliders, see Challenges 1 and 2.

A MacStarLogo Interface Window.

Command Center Window

This window is one place where you can type MacStarLogo commands. These commands are run as soon as you press **Return**. Commands you type here can be run even if the turtles are already running other commands. If you have a MacStarLogo project open, try typing **fd 5**. Make sure you press **Return** after the command. The small black circle you see to the right of the command lets you know that the command is running. You can run a command again by moving the cursor back up to that line and pressing **Return**.

The MacStarLogo Command Center Window.

The MacStarLogo Procedures Window.

Procedures Window

This window is where you write procedures for the turtles, patches, and the observer. A procedure is a set of instructions that teaches MacStarLogo how to do something new. This picture shows the procedures **go**, **check-patches**, **setup**, **wiggle**, and **clear-path**. You can define many procedures in your MacStarLogo projects. To learn more about writing your own procedures, see Challenge 3.

A Note on Writing Procedures

StarLogo differentiates explicitly among three characters—the observer, the turtles, and the patches—and commands need to be addressed to a particular character. In MacStarLogo, there is a single Procedures Window and a single Command Center. You do not need to specify which character should execute your instructions. Simply write your instructions in the Procedures Window or the Command Center, and MacStarLogo will figure out who the instruction is for and send it to the right character. For example, MacStarLogo knows that **fd** is a Turtle Command, and every time you use **fd** it asks the turtles to move forward.

Within the Challenges, the hints specify instructions that are "For this Character." In addition, the Challenges sometimes direct you to specify whether you want to **ask-turtles** or **ask-patches** to run a command. If you are using MacStarLogo, then you can safely ignore these distinctions. Simply use the commands in the Command Center or the Procedures Window, as desired, and *do not include the code* **ask-turtles** or **ask-patches**.

Though you do not have to separate Turtle, Observer, and Patch Commands, your MacStarLogo projects will run faster if you write procedures that do not mix commands for different characters.

Main Toolbar

The MacStarLogo Main Toolbar.

You use the **Toolbar** to create interface elements (like buttons, sliders, and monitors) and to choose other specialized toolbars and palettes (described at the end of this section). For example, to create a button you would click on the button icon in the **Toolbar**. For more on creating your own interface elements, see Challenge 2.

You can also look at the underlying instructions of an existing interface object. For example, if you choose the slider icon from the **Toolbar** and then click on an existing slider, you can see more about that slider. You can also inspect an interface element by choosing the arrow icon, pressing **Shift**, and double-clicking on the element.

Plot Window

You can create real-time graphs in this window as your MacStarLogo project is running. For more information on how to create your own graphs and use the **Plot Window**, see Challenge 8.

A MacStarLogo Plot Window.

Information Window

You can put explanatory notes, commentary, and instructions in the **Information Window**. This window is also a good place to provide some background on the project you developed and teach others how to experiment with your project.

A MacStarLogo Interface Window.

Paint and Color Toolbars

The **Paint Toolbar** and the **Color Toolbar** (see right) appear when you click on the paintbrush icon in the **Main Toolbar**. The **Paint Toolbar** allows you to select different types of drawing tools (like the pencil or the paintbucket) for drawing in the **Graphics Window**. When you paint, you can either place new turtles or simply color the patches, depending on which icon is selected on the **Color Toolbar**. With the **Color Toolbar** you can select the color that you want. The number associated with each color appears in the bottom of the **Color Toolbar**. For instance, in this picture you can see that gray is color number 5. For more information on colors, see http://www.media.mit.edu/macstarlogo/documentation/color.html. You can use the drawing tools in any project. For more information about how to use this feature of MacStarLogo, take a look at Challenge 2.

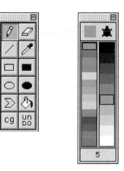

The MacStarLogo Paint Toolbar (left) and Color Toolbar (right).

Shapes Palette

This palette appears when you click on the last icon in the **Main Toolbar**. Currently, the **Shapes Palette** is available only in MacStarLogo. From here, you can create turtle shapes and assign them to particular turtles. Double-click on a shape to edit it. Notice that the shape name appears at the bottom of the **Shapes Palette**. When you have a shape selected, click on a turtle to assign the shape to the turtle. (Note: You must be in a project that displays turtle shapes—not just squares—to see the shapes. If you cannot see or alter the shapes in your project, go to **Edit** and open **Settings...** Change the patch size to 8 x 8 or 16 x 16 and reduce the size of your screen using the scroll bar until the box turns green. Now you will be able to manipulate turtle shapes in your project.)

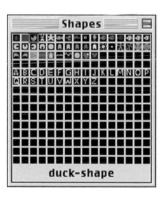

The MacStarLogo Shapes Palette.

Shapes are saved with each project. If you are interested in adding shapes to your projects, see the MacStarLogo Reference Manual for information: http://www.media.mit.edu/macstarlogo/documentation.

MACSTARLOGO NOTES FROM CHALLENGES

1 The buttons, which are divided into three different categories, appear in the **Interface Window** as shown to the right.

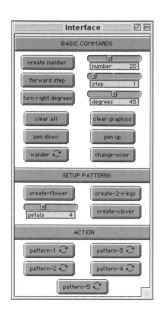

2 There is no text tool in MacStarLogo, so the sections of the projects are divided by three non-functional buttons.

3 The button editor looks like this in MacStarLogo:

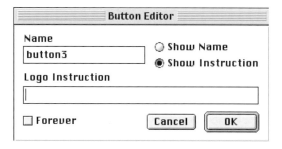

4 Since you do not need to tell MacStarLogo who a command is for, there is no need to specify if your **Logo Instruction** is for the turtles or the observer when you are creating buttons, writing procedures, or issuing commands. In the hints, you can ignore the "For this character" column.

5 The slider editor looks like this in MacStarLogo:

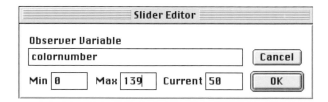

6 In MacStarLogo, the **Paint Tools** and **Color Palette** are both moveable toolbars; you can drag them to any place on the screen.

7 In MacStarLogo, this procedure should simply be written in the **Procedures Window**, since there are not separate **Command Centers** and **Procedure Windows** for the turtles and the observer.

8 If you are using the 68K version of MacStarLogo, you will notice that **pc-ahead** doesn't work. Go to the bottom of your **Procedures Window** and add the following procedure:

```
to pc-ahead
    output (pc-at dx dy)
end
```

This additional procedure defines **pc-ahead** and will work when typed in any project that uses **pc-ahead**.

9 The **Graphics Canvas** is a separate window, called the **Graphics Window**, in MacStarLogo.

10 To create a new project in MacStarLogo, select **New** from the **File** menu in the main menu bar across the top of the screen.

11 The **Procedures Window** is not combined with the **Control Center**. Rather, it is a separate window that usually sits behind the **Interface** and **Command Center Windows**. Clicking on it will bring it to the front of your screen. Alternatively, you can go to **Windows** in the menu bar and select **Procedures** to bring the **Procedures Window** to the front.

12 In the Java version of StarLogo, **crt** is an Observer Command, so it was omitted from this procedure to avoid confusion. In MacStarLogo you can write the **dance** procedure as:

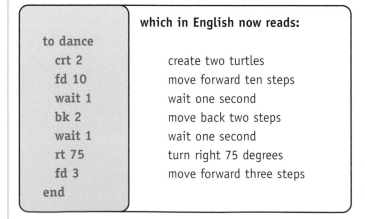

	which in English now reads:
to dance	
crt 2	create two turtles
fd 10	move forward ten steps
wait 1	wait one second
bk 2	move back two steps
wait 1	wait one second
rt 75	turn right 75 degrees
fd 3	move forward three steps
end	

13 In MacStarLogo, the distinction between Turtle Commands, Patch Commands, and Observer Commands is not formalized. Macintosh users should ignore the "For this character" column of the tables.

14 In MacStarLogo, the user does not need to specify which character is running a command. When you include a Turtle Command in an Observer Procedure, like **setup**, MacStarLogo automatically "asks" the turtles to run the command. **ask-turtles** and **ask-patches** do not exist in MacStarLogo. Just type **setpc blue** to change patch color to blue and **crt 100 seth 90** in your **setup** procedure.

15 Click on the value for **color**, type in a new value (or name) for **color** inside the **Turtle Monitor**, and then click on the value that you just typed to see the effect of your change.

16 In MacStarLogo, you need to make a turtle variable **partner**. Try creating a hundred moving red turtles with the turtle variable **partner** that run the following procedure:

```
to talk
    if turtles-here > 1 [setpartner one-of-turtles-here]
    setc-of partner blue
end
```

17 In MacStarLogo, the command **grab** does not exist. You can easily obtain the same results by creating an additional turtle variable called **partner** and using the following code in your procedure:

18 Use **if not (color = red) [statements]**, since **not=** is not a MacStarLogo command.

19 In MacStarLogo, the command **setplot-title** does not exist.

20 MacStarLogo users should type:

    breeds [*breed1 breed2*]

at the top of the **Procedures Window**.

21 In MacStarLogo,
    if breed = *breed1* [*statements*]
has **exactly** the same function as
    ask-*breed1* [*statements*].

```
if turtles-here > 1
    [setpartner one-of-turtles-here
      if (code1 = none)
      and (not ((code1-of other) = none))
      [setcode1 code1-of partner
      setnumber number + 1]
    ]
```

In English this reads:

If there is another turtle here,
    set your variable partner to that turtle's who number.
If you don't know code1
    and if the other turtle does know code1,
    then learn code1 and
    increase the number of words you know by one.

B

Collected Hints

If you want to...	Use these commands:	For this character:
Create turtles	The command **crt** *number* creates the number of turtles specified by *number*. Turtles are created in the center of the screen. Experiment with creating one or more turtles to discover their colors and headings.	
Move turtles	The command **fd** *step* moves each turtle forward the number of steps specified by *step*. Try: **fd 4**. Watch what happens when a turtle walks off the edge of the screen. The command **bk** *step* moves each turtle back the specified number of steps (but doesn't turn the turtle around).	
Change turtle direction	Turtle direction can be changed in several ways. One way is to rotate all of the turtles some number of degrees using the command **rt** *angle* where *angle* is the number of degrees you want the turtles to rotate clockwise. Try: **rt 45**. You can use **lt** *angle* in the same way. You can also set all turtles to the same heading using the command **seth** *direction* where *direction* is the heading on a compass (0 is towards the top of the screen) that you want the turtles facing. Try: **seth 45**.	
Change turtle color	Turtle color can be changed with the **setc** *newcolor* command, which changes all of the turtles to the color specified by *newcolor*. Note that *newcolor* can be simple color names (e.g., **red** or **blue**) or any number from 0 to 139. Try: **setc 105** or **setc blue**.	
Have turtles draw paths	Each turtle has a pen that can be in the up or down position. You can control this using the **pu** (**p**en **u**p) and **pd** (**p**en **d**own) commands. If a turtle's pen is down, it leaves a trail wherever it goes.	
Repeat a given statement multiple times	The statement **repeat** *times* **[***statements***]** will repeat the *statements* inside the square brackets the number of *times* you specify. For example, if you wanted a turtle to move forward 10 steps and turn right 30 degrees 5 times in a row you would use the statement: **repeat 5 [fd 10 rt 30]**.	depending on which one is able to execute *statements*
Clear all of the turtles and patches	The command **ca** removes all of the turtles and resets the patches to black.	
Remove all turtles from the world	The command **ct** kills all turtles but leaves the patches alone.	
Turn all of the patches black	The command **cg** clears the **Graphics Canvas**, by resetting all of the patches to black, but does not kill the turtles.	

CHALLENGE 2

If you want to...	Use these commands:	For this character:
Find out the patch color of the patch that a turtle is sitting on	The command **pc** returns the color of the patch that a turtle is on.	
Get the color of the patch directly in front of a turtle	The command **pc-ahead** returns the color of the patch directly in front of a turtle **8**.	
Find out the patch color of a specific patch	The command **pc-at** *x-coordinate y-coordinate* returns the patch color of that individual patch, relative to the character's position (the observer always "sits" at 0 0 while the turtles can be anywhere). Try typing **show pc-at 1 1** in both the **Turtle** and **Observer Command Centers** and see what happens.	
Generate a random number	The command **random** *number* will generate a random number from 0 to *number* – 1. For example, **random 3** will return 0, 1, or 2.	
Do something only if a certain condition is satisfied	The conditional **if** *condition* **[***statement***]** will execute *statement* if the stated *condition* is true. For example, the statement **if (pc = red) [rt 90]** will cause all turtles on red patches to turn 90 degrees to the right.	depending on whether Turtle or Observer Commands make up the *statement*

Have a turtle set the color of a patch that it is on	Use the command **stamp** *newcolor* to change the color of the patch to *newcolor*, where *newcolor* is either one of the basic color names or a color number.	
Change the color of the patches	Use the command **setpc** *newcolor*. For example, you could type **ask-patches [setpc blue]** or **ask-patches [setpc 101]**.	Note: This command must be called from within an **ask-patches** statement **14**.
Have new turtles "born" on a patch	Patches can create turtles using the **sprout [***statements***]** command. The *statements* are any commands you wish to give the newborn turtles. You can specify that only certain patches create turtles. For example: **ask-patches [if pc = 15 [sprout [setc blue]]]** creates blue turtles on patches whose color equals 15.	Note: This command must be called from within an **ask-patches** statement.
Have turtles "give birth" to new turtles	Turtles can create new turtles using the **hatch [***statements***]** command. The newborn turtle is identical to the "mother" turtle. You can give specific commands to the new turtle in the *statements*.	

If you want to...	Use these commands:	For this character:	
Create a new variable energy for all turtles	The statement **turtles-own [energy]** creates a new variable **energy** and allows you to use the set of commands that manipulate the turtles' **energy**.	This statement should be placed at the top of the **Turtle Procedures Pane**.	**CHALLENGE 5**
Set the value of energy for all turtles	The command **setenergy** *value* sets the variable **energy** to the *value* specified. Note that **setenergy** is one word.		
Increase the value of energy for all turtles	The command **setenergy energy + increase** adds the amount *increase* to the current energy level. Note that this is really the same as the last entry (**setenergy** *value*) with the *value* equal to the current **energy** plus an *increase*. Also, note the spaces on both sides of the plus sign.		
Do something to a turtle if its energy is above some value	Use the command **if energy > check [statements]** to cause turtles with an **energy** value greater than *check* to perform the *statements*.		

Multiply the energy of turtles who satisfy a certain condition	Use the statement
	  if *condition*
	    [setenergy energy * multiplier]
	to ask those turtles who satisfy the *condition* to multiply their **energy** by the *multiplier*. Try:
	  if color = blue [setenergy energy * 1.5].		

Do one thing if a certain condition is satisfied, and do something else if that condition is not satisfied	The conditional
	  ifelse *condition*
	    [statement1] [statement2]
	executes *statement1* if the stated condition is true and *statement2* if it is false. For example, the statement
	  ifelse color = blue
	    [rt 90] [lt 90]
	causes all blue turtles to turn right 90 degrees and all other turtles to turn left 90 degrees.
		depending on whether Turtle or Observer Commandsmake up *statement1* and *statement2*	**CHALLENGE 6**

Find out if there are any other turtles on a patch	The command **count-turtles-here** returns the number of turtles on a patch.		
Get the who number of another turtle that is on your patch	The command **one-of-turtles-here** returns the **who** number of another turtle on a patch, if there is another turtle present. If there are no other turtles present, then –1 is returned.		
Get the value of a variable from another turtle	Use the command **set***variable1* **(***variable2***-of one-of-turtles-here)** to get a variable value from another turtle. *variable1* is the name of the variable you are using to store the value of *variable2* from the other turtle. For example: **setotherage (age-of one-of-turtles-here)** stores the second turtle's **age** in the first turtle's variable **otherage**.	This code segment requires the following declaration of two turtle variables at the top of the **Turtle Procedures Pane**: **turtles-own [age otherage]**	

If you want to...	Use these commands:	For this character:
Talk to another turtle	The command **grab** *selectedturtle* [*statements*] allows a turtle to select a **partner** and then run the *statements*. *selectedturtle* is any command that returns a turtle's **who** number. A turtle only keeps his **partner** for the duration of the *statements*.	
Look at the variable of another turtle	The command *variable1***-of** *whonumber* allows a turtle to inspect another turtle's *variable1*. *whonumber* can be a number or a command that returns a **who** such as **partner** or **one-of-turtles-here**. For example: **if ((color-of partner) = blue) [setc red]** allows a turtle to check to see if his **partner** is blue and, if so, change his own **color** to red. The parentheses are required in this command.	
Change another turtle's variable	The command **set***variable2***-of** *whonumber* *newvalue* changes the other turtle's *variable2* to the *newvalue* you specify. For example, **setc-of 3 blue** changes the **color** of turtle three to blue.	
Execute commands if something is not true	Use a traditional **if** statement with the command **not=** to carry out instructions if a condition is not met. **if (color not= red) [***statement***]** runs the *statement* only if the turtle **color** is not red ⑱ .	
Define a variable that takes word values instead of numeric values	The statement **turtles-own [***variablename* [*word1 word2*]]] creates a new variable *variablename*, and allows you to set its value to *word1* or *word2*. For instance, you can create a variable **transport** that can take on four possible values: **turtles-own [transport [car boat truck train]]**	

CHALLENGE 7

If you want to...	Use these commands:	For this character:
Select which number pen you want to issue a command to	The command **pp***number* (where *number* is the number of the pen that you are selecting) tells StarLogo the pen to which you are going to issue a command. This command is followed by another command, such as **plot** or **ppreset**.	
Clear the whole plot	The command **clear-plot** resets the plot window.	
Clear the plot made by one of the pens	The command **ppreset** clears the plot made by whichever pen is currently selected.	
Choose the color of a plotting pen	The command **setppc** *color* sets the color of whichever pen is currently selected to the *color* that is specified.	
Set the plotting range on the x or y axes	The commands **setplot-xrange** *minimum maximum* and **setplot-yrange** *minimum maximum* set the x- and y-plot ranges to the *minimum* and *maximum* values specified.	
Plot the current value of a variable as the y value and the current time step as the x value	The command **plot** *value* directs the selected pen to **plot** a point on the graph on the y-axis at the *value* specified and on the x-axis at the next available value. By default the points are connected by a line.	
Plot individual points	The command **ppu** (for **p**lot **p**en **u**p) causes the plot pen to draw x's instead of plotting a continuous line. Use **ppd** to switch back to a continuous line.	
Put a title on your plot	The command **setplot-title "***name***"** sets the plot title to *name* ⑲ .	
Label the plot axes	The commands **setplot-xlabel "***x-axis name***"** and **setplot-ylabel "***y-axis name***"** allow you to put labels on the axes of your plot.	

CHALLENGE 8

If you want to...	Use these commands:	For this character:
Head towards a point on the Graphics Canvas	The command **seth towards** *x-coordinate y-coordinate* makes turtles turn in the direction of the *x-coordinate* and *y-coordinate* specified. For example: **seth towards 0 0** makes all of the turtles turn in the direction of the center of the screen (which is at location 0,0).	
Find the location of another turtle	The commands **xcor-of** *whonumber* and **ycor-of** *whonumber* return the corresponding x-coordinate and y-coordinate of *whonumber*.	
Find the coordinates of the current mouse location	The commands **mouse-xcor** and **mouse-ycor** return the x-coordinate and y-coordinate of the mouse as long as it is on the **Graphics Canvas**. For example the Turtle Command **seth towards mouse-xcor mouse y-cor** points turtles **towards** the current mouse location.	
Find out whether the mouse button is pressed	The command **mouse-down?** returns true if the mouse button is down and false if it is not.	

If you want to...	Use these commands:	For this character:
Create a new breed for all turtles	The statement **breeds [*breedname*]** creates a new breed *breedname*, and allows you to use a special set of commands to address only *breedname*. Try: **breeds [lions]**. This statement should be placed at the top of the **Turtle Procedures Pane**.	
Create turtles of a particular breed	The command **create-*breed1 number*** creates the number of turtles of type *breed1* specified by *number*. For example, to create 12 turtles of type lions you would use the command **create-lions 12**.	
Change the breed of a turtle from one breed to another	Use the command **setbreed** *breed2* to change an existing turtle from its current breed to *breed2*.	
Ask all lions to do something	The command **if breed = lions [*statements*]** instructs all of the **lions** to perform the *statements*.	
Ask all lions to do something	The command **ask-lions [*statements*]** instructs all of the **lions** to perform the *statements*.	
Count the number of turtles in a breed	The command **count-*breed1*** returns the number of *breed1* turtles alive at that moment and can be used with any breed that you have created.	

Common StarLogo Error Messages

As you learn to build models in StarLogo you, like all of us, will encounter numerous StarLogo error messages. While not all of the error messages are friendly, most of them are reasonably helpful if you take the time to read them. Don't click **OK** before trying to decode the message.

In this table you will find many of the most common error messages. In each message, the key phrase has been highlighted. If you get an error that is not listed in the table, look for a related error message using the italicized phrases. The fix for your error is likely to be conceptually similar to the fix listed in a related message.

This procedure...	generates this error message...	because...	To correct the error...
to go **crt 10** **fd 20** **end**	*"turtle can't call a primitive observer command* crt in the procedure named go in the turtle procedures page"	typing this **go** procedure in the **Turtle Procedures Pane** generates an error since **crt** is an Observer Command, not a Turtle Command, so it can only be used in the **Observer Procedures Pane**.	put **crt 10** in a separate **setup** procedure in the **Observer Procedures Pane**.
to go **crt 10** **fd 20** **end**	*"observer can't call a primitive turtle command* fd in the procedure named go in the observer procedures page"	typing this **go** procedure in the **Observer Procedures Pane** generates an error since **fd** is a Turtle Command, not an Observer Command, so it can only be used in the **Turtle Procedures Pane** or inside **ask-turtles** in the **Observer Procedures Pane**.	put **fd 20** in a separate **go_turtles** procedure in the **Turtle Procedures Pane**, or type **ask-turtles [fd 20]** in the **Observer Procedures Pane**.
to go **fd 10** **seth** **end**	*"not enough inputs* to seth in the procedure named go in the turtle procedures page"	**seth** needs a value (the "input" in the error message) after it that tells the turtles what to set their headings to.	insert a value after **seth**, such as **seth 45**.
to go **fd 10** **seth** **slider_name** **end**	"turtle *doesn't know how to* slider_name in the procedure named go in the turtle procedures page"	the slider **slider_name** has not yet been created and therefore cannot return a value.	simply create a slider called **slider_name** and set its value to the heading you would like the turtles to assume.
to go **fd 10** **setc (45 * 2** **end**	*"unbalanced parentheses* in procedure go starting at line 1 in the turtle procedures page"	every open parenthesis needs a closed parenthesis.	add the closed parenthesis to the command: **setc (45 * 2)**

This procedure...	generates this error message...	because...	To correct the error...

to go
  fd 10
  if color = red
seth 270 fd 1
end
	"seth is *not an instruction list* in the procedure named go in the turtle procedures page"	after the condition of the **if** statement (**color = red**) the program is looking for a list of instructions that are inside square brackets. Without square brackets, the turtles who meet the condition do not know what to do.	add square brackets around the list of instructions that you want the turtles to run if they are red:
			  if color = red [seth 270 fd 1]

to go
  if
    random 3 = 1
    [fd 2]
end
	"*false is not an integer* in turtle #99 while running instruction random"	StarLogo evaluates mathematical expressions first. In this case, the command is evaluated as **random (3 = 1)**, generating "false" in the error, since 3 never equals 1. If you want to change the order of evaluation, you need to use parentheses. It is a good idea to use parentheses whenever you use **random**.	add parentheses around the part of the expression that you want to evaluate first:
			  if (random 3) = 1 [fd 2]

to go
  sprout [setc blue]
end
	"*observer can't call a primitive patch command* sprout in the procedure named go in the observer procedures page"	each patch command should be written in the **Observer Procedures Pane**, inside of an **ask-patches** statement.	place the patch commands inside an **ask-patches** command:
			  ask-patches [sprout [setc blue]]

to clone
  hatch
  fd 1
end
	"fd is *not an instruction list* in the procedure named clone in the turtle procedures page"	after the **hatch** command, StarLogo is looking for a list of instructions to give to the newly hatched turtles. Without square brackets, the program is unable to distinguish that list.	place the instructions for all newly hatched turtles inside of square brackets after the **hatch** command:
			  hatch [fd 1]

to start
  setage 10
end
	"turtle *doesn't know how* to setage in the procedure named start in the turtle procedures page"	you need to define a variable, using **turtles-own**, before you can use it in a project.	add the statement
			  turtles-own [age]
			at the very top of the **Turtle Procedures Pane** to create the turtle variable **age**. Now you will be able to use **age** in any Turtle Procedure.

to grow
  setage + 1
end
	"*not enough inputs* to + in the procedure named grow in the turtle procedures page"	you haven't told the turtles what they should add **1** to. If you want **age** to increase by one, you need to add **1** to the existing value of **age**.	if you want the new value of the variable to depend on the previous value of the variable, make sure that you include the variable in your calculation for the new value. For instance,
			  setage age + 1
			will increment the value of **age** by one each time the command is run.

to go
  seth
  towards 3
end
	"*not enough inputs* to towards in the procedure named go in the turtle procedures page"	the **towards** command needs both an x-coordinate and a y-coordinate for the turtles to head **towards**. Also, make sure that you specify both coordinates if your turtles are heading towards other turtles (using **xcor-of** *who* and **ycor-of** *who*).	if you want the turtles to head **towards** the point **3, 4** make sure that you specify both coordinates:
			  seth towards 3 4

This procedure...	generates this error message...	because...	To correct the error...

to decide
  if pc-ahead = blue
    [rt 90]
  else
    [lt 90]
end
	"turtle *doesn't know how* to else in the procedure named decide in the turtle procedures page"	the **ifelse** command is one word. The statements to be run if the condition (**pc-ahead = blue**) is true are placed in the first set of square brackets. The statements to be run if the condition is false are placed in the second set of square brackets.	rewrite the **ifelse** command as a single word, followed first by the condition, then by the statements to be run if the condition is true, and finally by the statements to be run if the condition is false:
			  ifelse pc-ahead = blue
			    [rt 90]
			    [lt 90]

to decide
  if color = blue
          or red
  [fd 1]
end
	no error is generated but all turtles will move forward, regardless of their color	you need to write out each condition fully in order for it to be evaluated. When the second condition is a fragment that depends on the first condition, the command will not run as expected.	amend the second condition so that it is a complete "logical sentence" instead of a fragment that depends on part of the earlier condition:
			  if (color = red) or
			    (color = blue) [fd 1]
			Now, only **red** or **blue** turtles will move **fd 1**.

to talk
  grab
  one-of-turtles-here
[if
  age-of partner = 2
    [fd 1]]
end
	"false is not an integer in turtle #16 while running instruction %gett-of"	StarLogo evaluates mathematical expressions first. In this case, the command is evaluated as **age-of (partner = 2)**, generating the "false" in the error statement. If you want to change the order of evaluation, you need to use parentheses. It is a good idea to use parentheses whenever you use **variable-of** or **partner**.	add parentheses to the **if** statement so that the turtle *first* checks to see what the **age** of his **partner** is and *then* checks if that **age** is equal to **2**:
			  if (age-of partner) = 2
			    [fd 1]

turtles-own
[gender
  [male female age]
	"*unfinished turtles-own* on line 1 in the turtle procedures page"	both the **turtles-own** statement and the list of acceptable words as values for **gender** need complete sets of square brackets. Make sure that you always close the brackets for the list of words before you type the next variable.	change the **turtles-own** statement so that the brackets are balanced and correctly reflect the acceptable word values for gender:
			  turtles-own
			    [gender [male female] age]

to graph
  pp1 count-color
red
end
	"observer *doesn't know what to do with* count-color in the procedure named graph in the observer procedures page"	after you choose a plot pen (using **pp1**), you need to tell StarLogo to **plot** the specified value (in this case, **count-color red**).	simply add the command **plot** to the statement:
			  pp1 plot count-color red

to go
  fd 1
  ask-tigers [
    setc green]
end
	"turtle can't call a primitive observer command %ask-breeds in the procedure named go in the turtle procedures page"	only the observer can use the command **ask-tigers**. In the **Turtle Procedures Pane**, you must use the turtle command **if breed = *breedname*** instead.	if you want the **tigers** to do something from within a Turtle Procedure, replace
			  ask-tigers [setc green]
			with
			  if breed = tigers [setc green]

Bibliography

Axelrod, R. (1984). *The Evolution of Cooperation*. New York: Basic Books.

Bedini, S. (1964). *The Role of Automata in the History of Technology, Technology and Culture* (pp. 24–42): University of Chicago Press.

Booth Sweeney, L., & Meadows, D. (forthcoming 2001). *The Whole Systems Thinking Playbook, Revised and Expanded Edition*. Waltham, MA: Pegasus Communications.

Brosterman, N. (1997). *Inventing Kindergarten*. New York: Harry N. Abrams.

Byington, S. (1997). Simulating population growth. *American Biology Teacher, 59*(6), 353.

Colella, V. (2000). Participatory Simulations: Building collaborative understanding through immersive dynamic modeling. *Journal of the Learning Sciences, 9*(4), 471-500.

Colella, V., Klopfer, E., & Resnick, M. (1999). StarLogo Community of Learners Workshop. Logo Exchange, *Journal of the ISTE Special Interest Group for Logo-Using Educators, 17*(2), 20-22.

Confrey, J., & Doerr, H. (1994). Student modelers. *Interactive Learning Environments, 4*(3), 199–217.

Dewdney, A. (1996). *200% Of Nothing: An Eye-Opening Tour Through the Twists and Turns of Math Abuse and Innumeracy*. New York: John Wiley & Sons.

diSessa, A. (1986). Artificial worlds and real experience. *Instructional Science, 14*, 207–227

Feurzeig, W., & Roberts, N. (Eds.). (1999). *Modeling and Simulation in Precollege Science and Mathematics Education*. New York: Springer-Verlag.

Fretwell, S., & Lucas, H. (1970). On territorial behaviour and other factors influencing habitat distribution in birds. *Acta Biotheoretica, 19*, 16–36.

Huff, D., & Geis, I. (1993). *How to Lie With Statistics*. New York: W. W. Norton.

Kafai, Y., & Ching, C. (1998). *Talking science through design: Children's science discourse within software design activities*. Paper presented at the International Conference of the Learning Sciences (ICLS), Atlanta, GA.

Kolodner, J., Crismond, D., Gray, J., Holbrook, J., & Puntambekar, S. (1998). *Learning by design from theory to practice*. Paper presented at the ICLS, Atlanta, GA.

Kolodner, J., & Nagel, K. (1999). *The design discussion area: A collaborative learning tool in support of learning from problem-solving and design activities*. Paper presented at the Computer Supported Collaborative Learning (CSCL) Conference, Palo Alto, CA.

Levin, S. (1999). *Fragile Dominion: Complexity and the Commons*. Reading, MA: Perseus Books.

Lotka, A. (1956). *Elements of Mathematical Biology*. New York: Dover. (Originally published as *Elements of Physical Biology* in 1925)

Papert, S. (1980). *Mindstorms: Children, Computers, and Powerful Ideas*. New York: Basic Books, Inc.

Puntambekar, S., & Kolodner, J. (1998). *The design diary: Development of a tool to support students learning science by design*. Paper presented at the ICLS, Atlanta, GA.

Resnick, M. (1994). *Turtles, Termites, and Traffic Jams: Explorations in Massively Parallel Microworlds*. Cambridge, MA: MIT Press.

Resnick, M., Bruckman, A., & Martin, F. (1996). Pianos not stereos: Creating computational construction kits. *Interactions, 3*(6), 41-50.

Resnick, M., & Wilensky, U. (1998). Diving into complexity: Developing probabilistic decentralized thinking through role-playing activities. *The Journal of the Learning Sciences, 7*(2), 153-172.

Roughgarden, J., Bergman, A., Shafir, S., & Taylor, C. (1996). Adaptive Computation in Ecology and Evolution: A Guide for Future Research. In R. Belew & M. Mitchell (Eds.), *Adaptive Individuals in Evolving Populations: Models and Algorithms* (pp. 25-30). Reading, MA: Addison-Wesley.

Schelling, T. (1978). *Micromotives and Macrobehavior*. New York: Norton.

Shaffer, D. (1998). *The pedagogy of the digital studio: Learning through collaboration, expression and construction*. Paper presented at the ICLS, Atlanta, GA.

Sterman, J. (2000). *Business Dynamics: Systems Thinking and Modeling for a Complex World*. Boston, MA: Irwin McGraw-Hill.

Talsma, V. (2000). *Scientific understandings revealed by students' computer models of a stream: A trickle or a flood?* Paper presented at the ICLS, Ann Arbor, MI.

Tufte, E. (1983). *The Visual Display of Quantitative Information*. Cheshire, CT: Graphics Press.

Tufte, E. (1990). *Envisioning Information*. Cheshire, CT: Graphics Press.

Tufte, E. (1997). *Visual Explanations*. Cheshire, CT: Graphics Press.

Volterra, V. (1926). Fluctuations in the abundance of a species considered mathematically. *Nature, 188*, 558–560.

Wilensky, U., & Stroup, W. (2000). *Networked gridlock: Students enacting dynamic phenomena with the HubNet architecture*. Paper presented at the ICLS, Ann Arbor, MI.

Note: Links to all of the curriculum standards cited in Chapter 5 are available on the Adventures web site at http://www.media.mit.edu/starlogo/adventures.